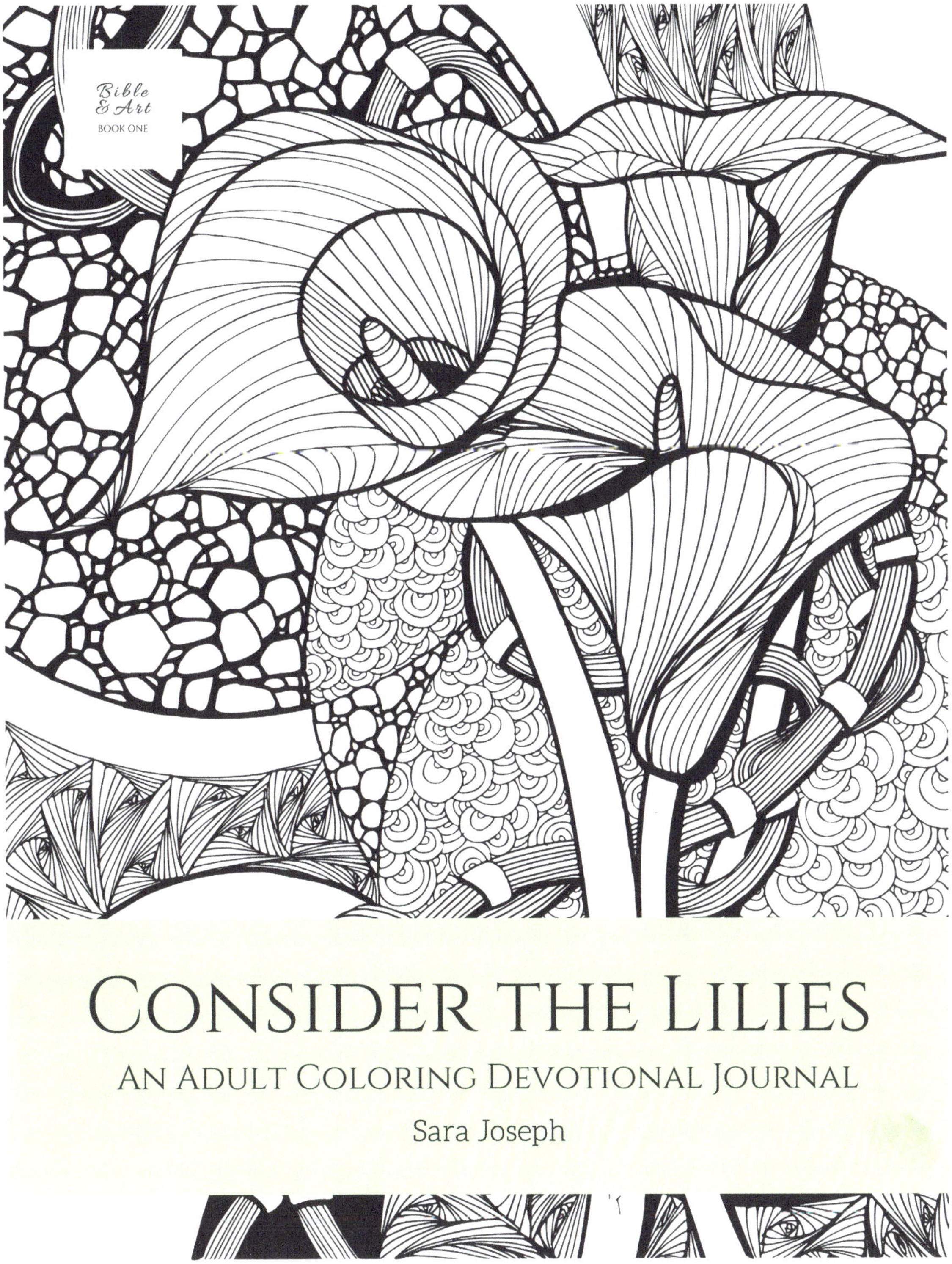

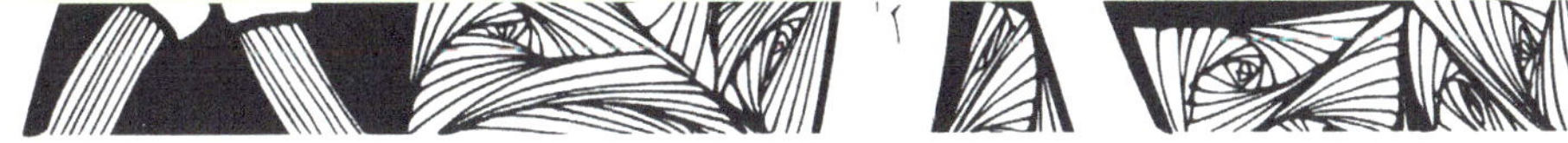

Consider the Lilies

An Adult Coloring Devotional Journal

Sara Joseph

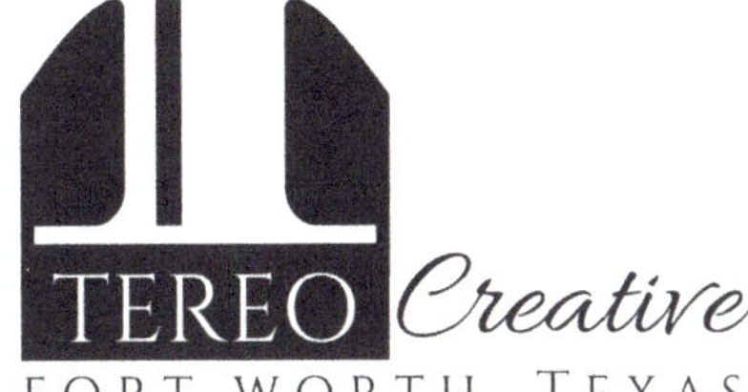

www.christian-artist-resource.com

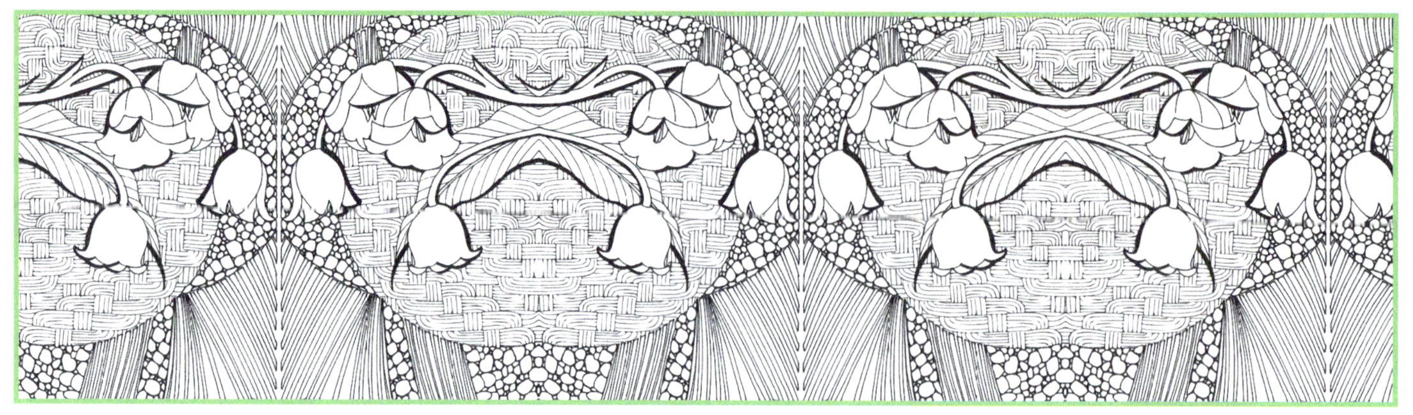

Consider the Lilies
an Adult Coloring Devotional Journal

Bible & Art Series: Book One

Copyright © 2016 Sara Joseph

All Rights Reserved

Author Website: www.christian-artist-resource.com

Email: sarajoseph@christian-artist-resource.com

All Scripture quotations are taken from the Holy Bible, King James Version, public domain.

ISBN 978-0-9973673-0-0 (Paperback)

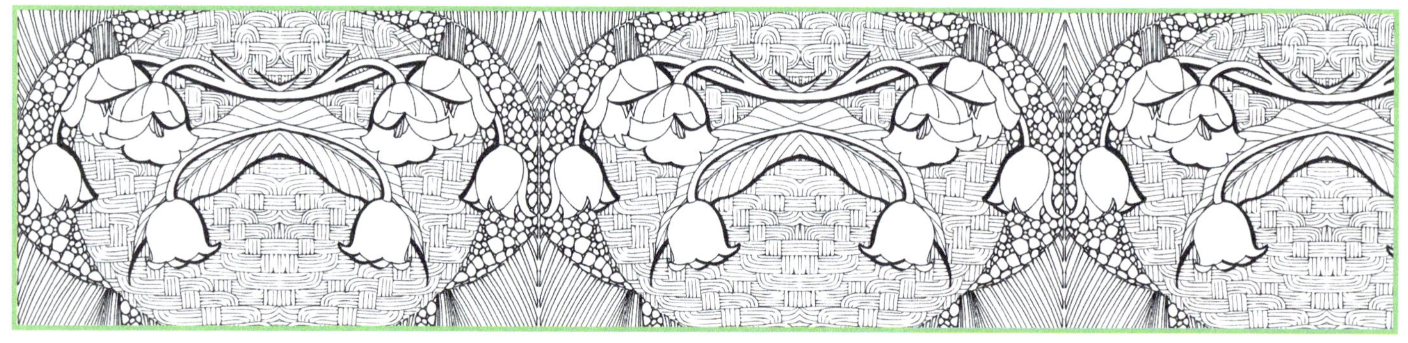

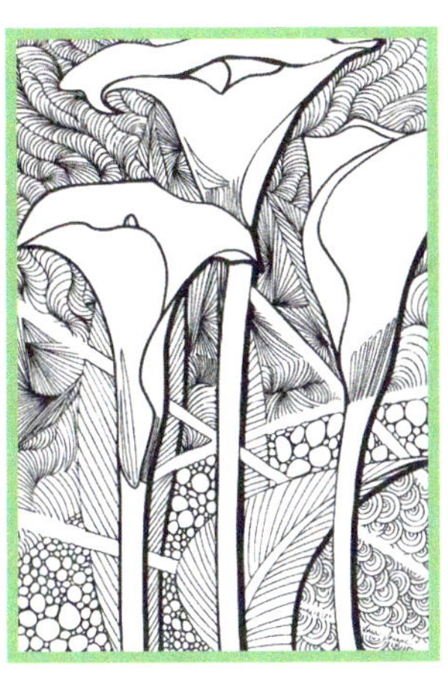

This book is dedicated to God, my Father,
the Author of all beauty,
and to my Savior and Lord, Jesus Christ.
His words offer life to whosoever will believe.
It is His will that we live carefree,
sublime lives like the lilies of the field.

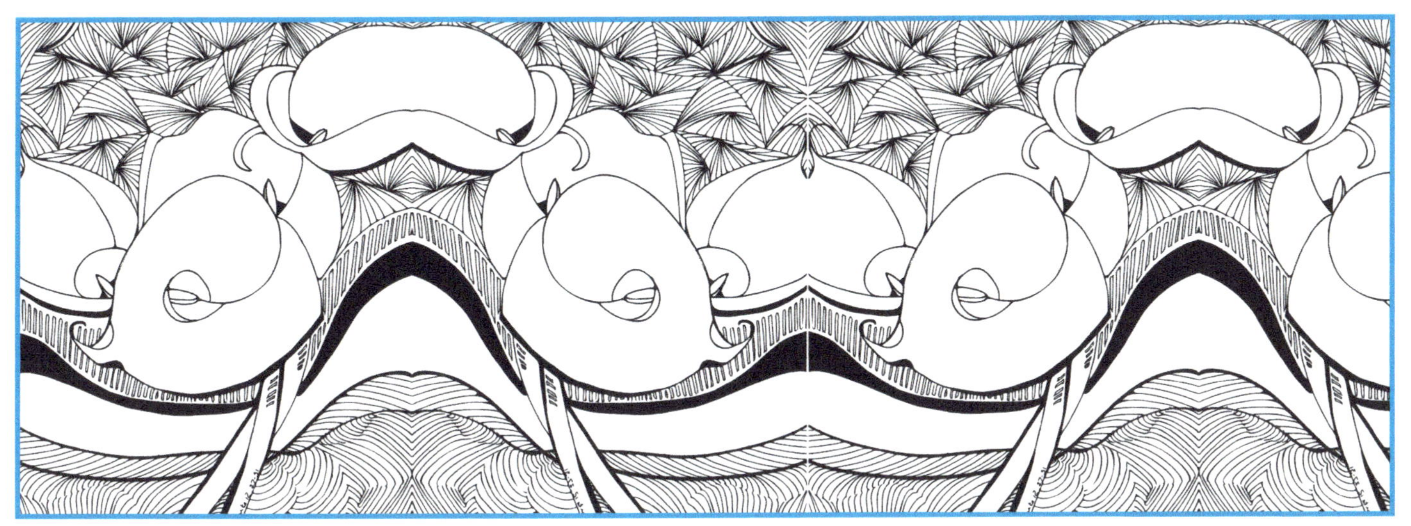

This Journal Belongs To:

____

Begun On

____

Completed On

____

*"Being confident of this very thing, that he which hath begun a
good work in you will perform it until the day of Jesus Christ."*
Philippians 1:6

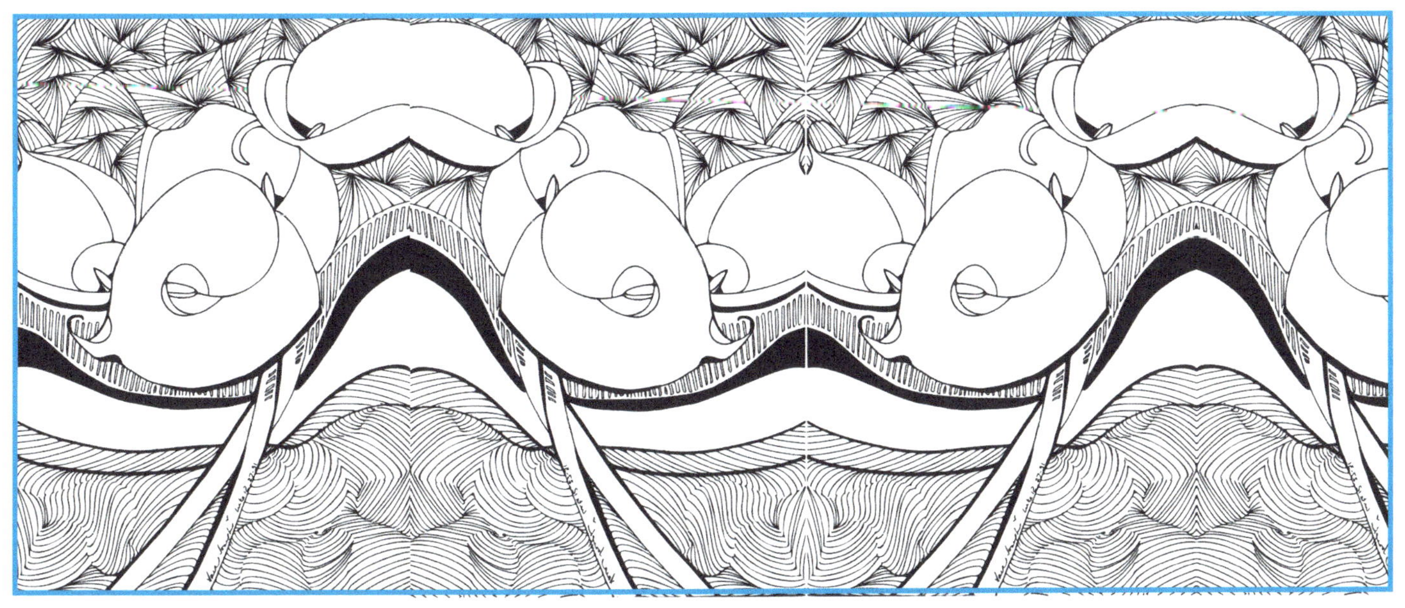

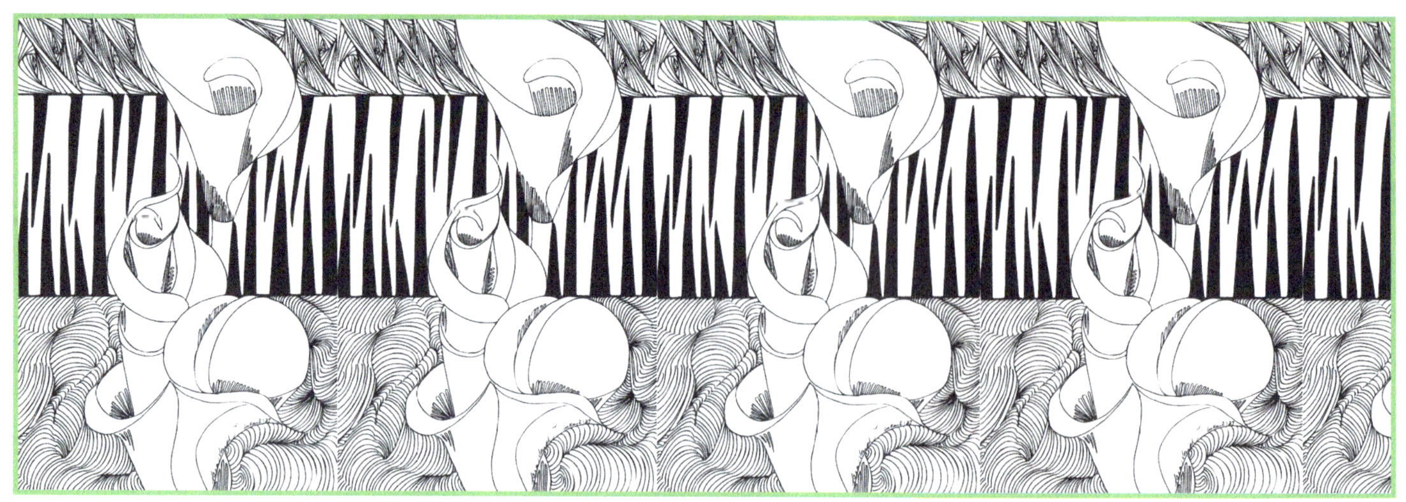

Table of Contents

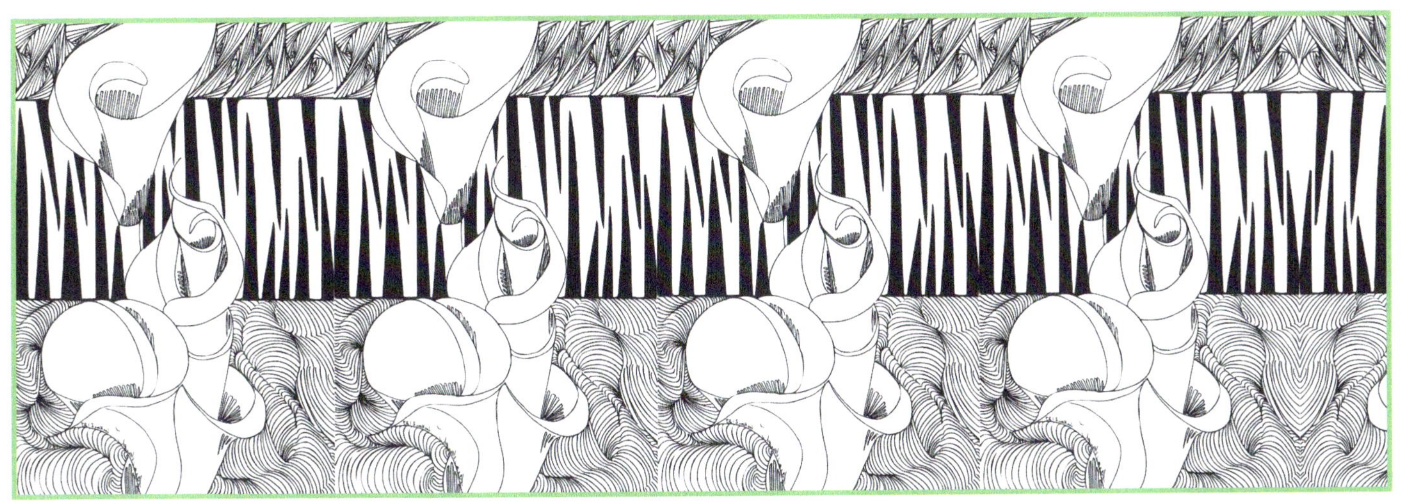

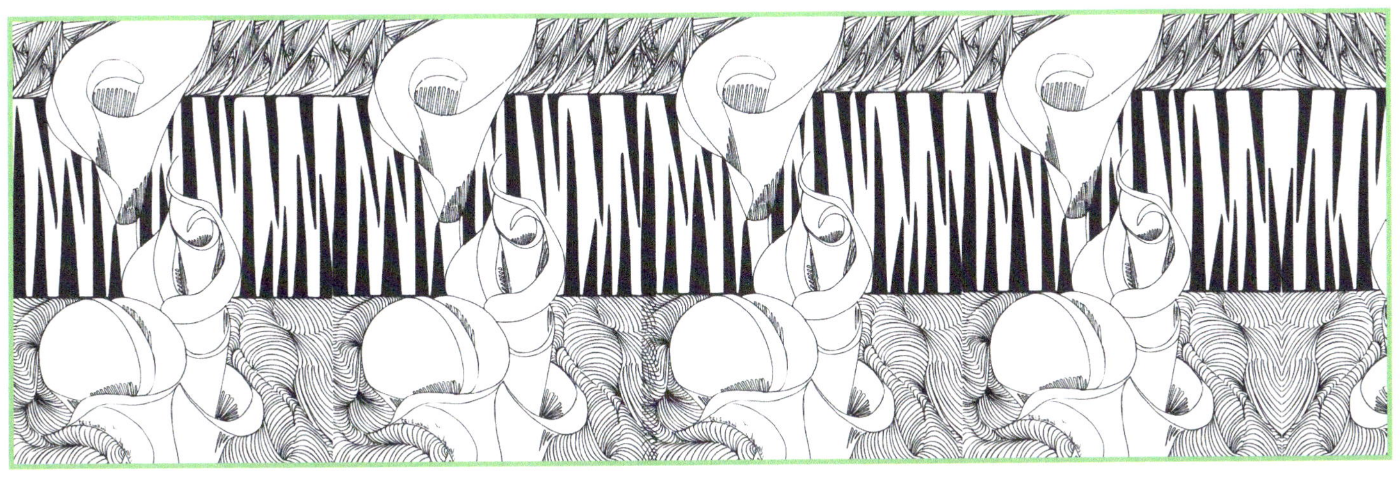

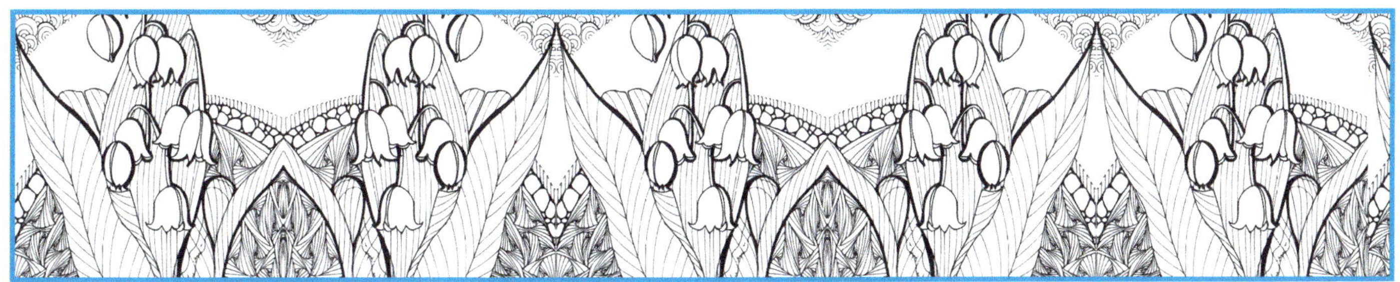

An Unusual Journal

As paper repositories that receive our unvarnished selves, journals have been treasured for centuries. They don't argue back, offer advice, criticize, or otherwise annoy us for being who we are. In them, thoughts that would otherwise float aimlessly are allowed to spill unchecked. They record meals enjoyed and places visited, hide opinions that no one else would care about, or just capture the daily tramp of time that we call life.

Regardless of content, journals are invariably guarded and cherished by those who keep them. No harsh critical voice is permitted access to their pages—not even our own. Dreams, wild ideas, and aspirations have room to nest, hatch, and find wings. Their pages also serve as a toasty incubator for flights of fancy, which may lie dormant for years before being revived or dismissed.

Journals can also occasionally be mind-numbingly dull, even for those who write in them. "I slipped and fell and I'm sore in places I did not know could hurt" or "Can a day be any more blah than this one?" don't exactly make for thrilling reading, but no one can deny that they are authentic sentiments of the moment.

Art journals are different. Vivid with color, they record the creative ideas of visually inclined people who use the emptiness of their pages to explore concepts in line and shape. For those who are not so skilled with brush and ink, a coloring journal offers a satisfying alternative. Coloring is a creative activity that ushers in calm, providing the quiet triumph of control in an otherwise unruly world. A postiive outcome is anticipated even before beginning. It is a return to childhood, when life was no more complicated than deciding whether pink or yellow was your favorite color. If you abandoned coloring a long time ago, you may find yourself surprised at how much fun it can be as an adult. Why not enjoy a welcome break from juggling the complex responsibilities of a grown-up life by picking up a pencil and coloring?

Combining the quiet creativity of coloring with meditating on God's Word is the purpose of this journal. Quiet time with Jesus, the Bible and a journal is precious. There is no better way to be renewed and strengthened.

Responding to the prompts, reading the poetry, and contemplating the Scriptures while coloring will help you silence the worries of the day so that Jesus can teach you His truths. There is plenty of room for you to ask Him questions and to journal His responses and your thoughts. His Holy Spirit has promised to guide you into all truth. Expect to be guided.

The prompts I have included in some pages are those I asked myself when I contemplated these verses. Your responses to them will be different from mine, based on your unique life experience. Be honest and document your journey to understanding.

Each of the ink drawings in this book is a painstaking labor of love. Unlike the computer-generated drawings of other coloring books, these hand-drawn images bear the imperfections of human endeavor. Please ignore ink that overstepped its bounds and look kindly upon any wobbly lines that you may spot. They are reflective of our flawed human condition. I yearn and strive for perfection, as I'm sure you do, and consistently fall short of it. The occasional errant streak of ink on paper only warms me to thoughts of my perfect God, who sent His perfect Son for flawed me! Yet He loves us so much that He corrects our errors, picks us up when we stumble, and urges us on our journey to perfection.

Therefore when you color a page and the result does not look as you envisioned it, be gentle with yourself. Treasure the process, since by it you will surely grow.

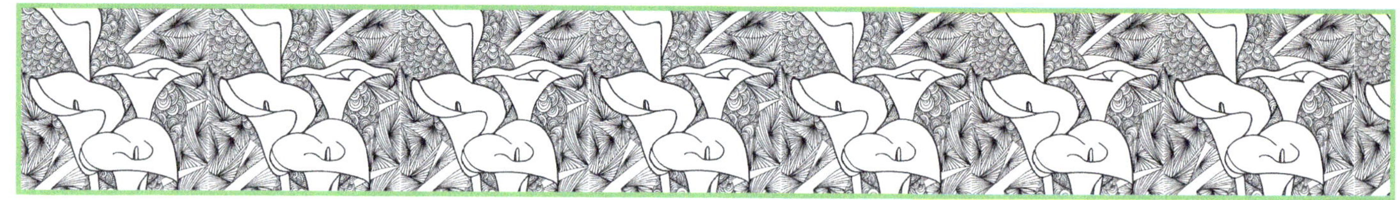

BEFORE YOU COLOR

These prayerfully created drawings are the fruit of my reflecting on the Scriptures lingered upon in this journal. In my conversations with God while drawing, I learned much I needed to know. As you fill in the colors while meditating on the verses, you will learn too. I promise you that you will receive insight for your specific needs and challenges. Act upon all that you are taught, and your life will certainly never be the same!

Here are some things to think about before you begin:

❧ **This book is less about coloring and more about communing with God and learning from Him.**

❧ Although this is a journal, its pages are deliberately not dated. So don't feel guilty if you miss a day; there are no appointments to keep. You choose the time and place, and add a date to help you reminisce one day in the future. The words you commit to paper will cause you to marvel at changes only He could have wrought in you!

❧ Welcome the Lord's presence whenever you sit down to this journal, and fill its pages with whatever He teaches you. There is plenty of room for color, thoughts, insights, and yes, dates, recorded without guilt.

❧ Don't allow the familiarity of these sacred words to lull you into complacency. God can reveal insights you never knew existed. He will ensure that they are pertinent to you if you come before Him in faith, expectantly.

❧ **Color with colored pencils.** Prismacolor pencils are recommended. They come in a wide variety of luscious colors in artist-grade options like Soft Core, Verithin®, Art Stix® and others like these. Softer than other coloring pencils, they require less pressure and will reward your efforts with vivid, even colors. They are consequently more expensive than other brands. The results are well worth the difference in cost. This is a sacred journey, so I encourage you to bring excellence to every aspect of it. The choice, however, is yours to make.

❧ Gel pens and markers are not a good idea because they will bleed to the page below. If you just can't help yourself, put a sturdy piece of cardboard or something else to absorb the excess ink and protect the pages below. The back of each drawing has deliberately been left blank for this reason. Make sure you use a light touch when using pens; otherwise ink-sodden paper can tear. This paper is best suited to pencils.

❧ It may be tempting to remove a page that you're really thrilled about in order to frame it or to grace your refrigerator with it. I would recommend that you don't do so. Removing pages would cause the journal to lack vital information about your growth and transformation. I deliberately did not include perforations because I know that you will be too pleased with the journey to deface a mile marker on the way. I pray that your complete journal becomes a record so precious that you will prize it in its entirety!

❧ You do not have to color every little space if that is overwhelming to you. Look for the larger shapes and unify the colors in those. If, on the other hand, you find the little spaces fascinating, then think of each coloring page as you would a panel of stained glass. Fill in the small spaces that make up the leaves in multiple shades of green or the background shapes in as varied a color palette as you choose. Select your favorite colors, experiment, play, and enjoy coloring the drawings in this book. Look online on the book page of *Consider the Lilies: An Adult Coloring Devotional Journal* on www.amazon.com to see how others have colored these same pages if you are seeking inspiration.

❧ Above all, keep the verses in mind as you color. May they whisper their truths to transform your life!

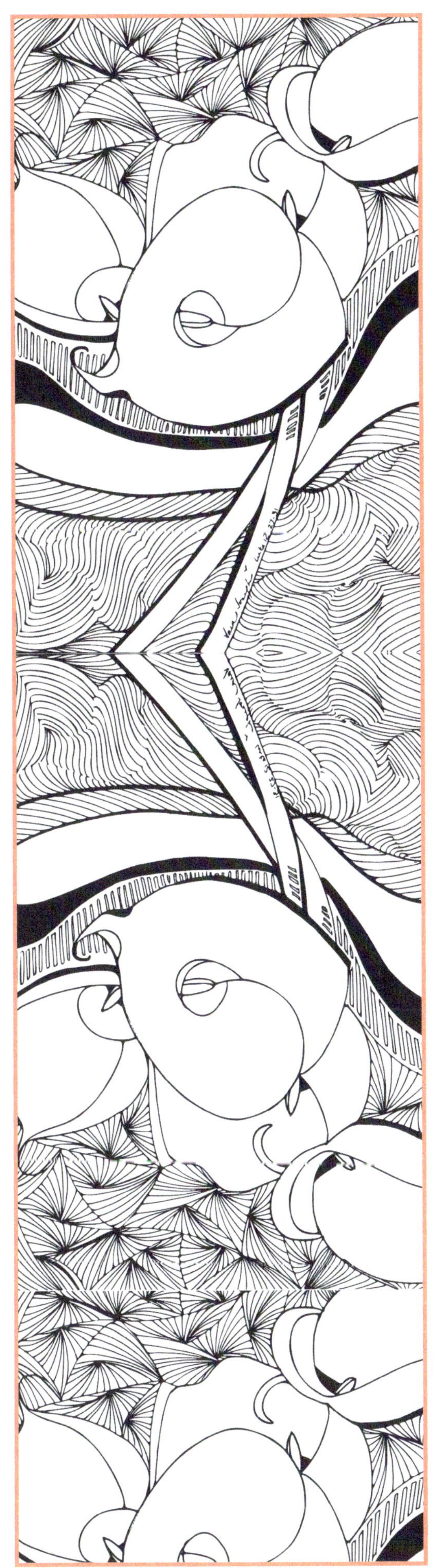

PEACE

In our hectic lives, pausing, while sometimes seemingly impossible, becomes an act of beauty. "Peace," we hear the Lord say, and yet we struggle to enter into that sanctuary of rest. Even when stilling our bodies, peace seems elusive. Our harried minds churn on, regurgitating anxieties and urging fruitless action.

Entering into a state of peace is as wonderful as stepping into a holy place, yet for most it's a struggle to even find the door.

As an artist who has tasted the peace that passes understanding, I know that an act of creativity has the potential to work the necessary magic. Every time I step into my studio, I enter a haven of tranquility, where creativity is nurtured and ideas have a chance to breathe. There, I enjoy God's presence and bask in His peace.

In the silence of coloring, you too can enter that state of rest and renew your mind with the Word. Listen to the voice of the Holy Spirit as you think about the verse that accompanies the drawings. God can show you depths of truth in His word that you have not perceived before. Scripture possesses the power to transform your life from within as you meditate and act in faith. Surrender willingly to the process.

As you spend time in this journal, hold His Word in your thoughts, asking for insight and understanding. He has a wonderful way of shining a spotlight on the very truth we need to live victorious lives. Renewing your mind with the Word takes time. What better way to spend time than by thinking visually while feasting on the Word as you do so!

Can you do both—journal thoughts and color? Absolutely! Switch back and forth as you work. Make your coloring endeavor more than just a pleasurable activity.

Each illustration can serve as a personal bookmark reminding you of a specific season of your life. Infuse these pages with memory and meaning: the memory of a journey of growth and the riches of lessons learned from these truths. Even as you enjoy the beauty of your very own colored work, date your thoughts and drawings and save them as your personal visual record.

When you've made these drawings vibrant with your favorite colors, may you have journeyed to somewhere new—a place of greater confidence in Jesus, strengthened with unshakable faith in His Word!

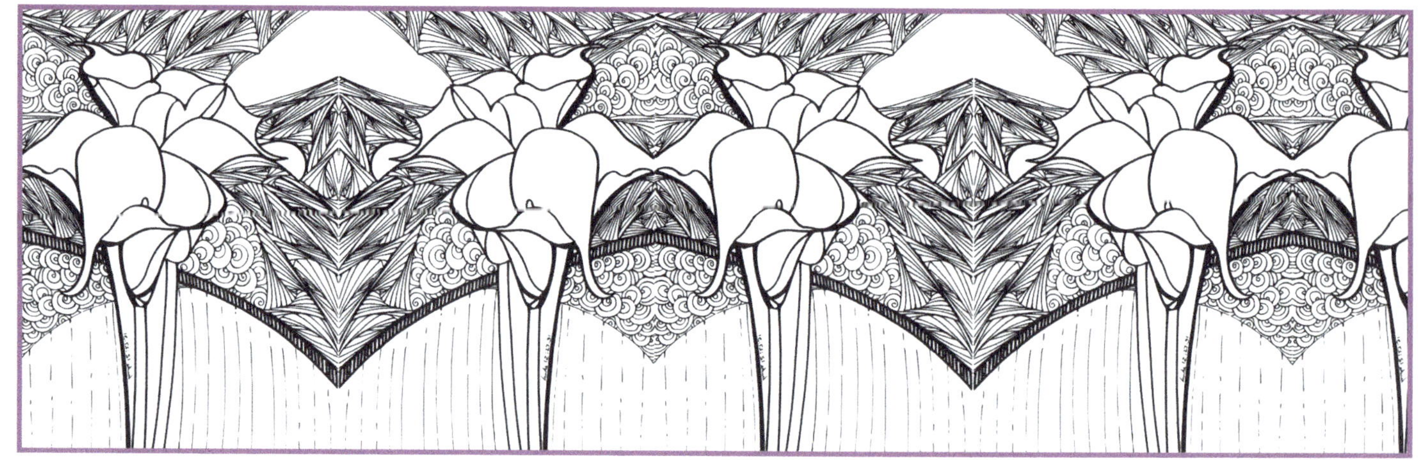

Live, Don't Just Register a Pulse!

I once watched a boa constrictor do its sinuous dance of death at a zoo event for kids. Noiselessly curving up the handler's body, it wrapped itself in graceful, deadly coils around its human prey. Boa constrictors kill by cutting off the victim's blood supply and interrupting life-giving circulation to vital organs. Continuously monitoring the heartbeat of its prey, the boa can precisely identify the moment of death. All it takes is a couple of twists and life is silently snuffed out. Fully aware of that, the handler firmly peeled the snake off his body well before it posed a real threat. Little girls squealed and shuddered, while the boys were fascinated.

Life's challenges can sometimes feel just as stifling. Worry works like that boa, steadily applying pressure, slowing your heartbeat until you may still be alive even if you no longer register a pulse. How unlike the life that God intended for you!

Jesus understood the deadly power of worry. The beautiful imagery that He uses in Luke 12:27-32 and Matthew 6:28-33 is the theme of this journal. It is my prayer that as you work through these pages, you will develop resilience and muster the courage to fight being squeezed by life's challenges.

God knows we live in troubled times. Yet He tells us not to worry, which is a command we ought to take very seriously.

Interestingly enough, the boa constrictor has more difficulty killing ectotherms, animals like lizards and snakes that rely on external heat to regulate their body temperatures. Can we not also learn to rely on the external help that God so readily provides if we but trust Him for it? Would we not grow stronger if our strength was not based on our limited resources but rather His infinite supply?

Lilies will teach us how.

So forget about the constrictor and let's consider the lily, shall we?

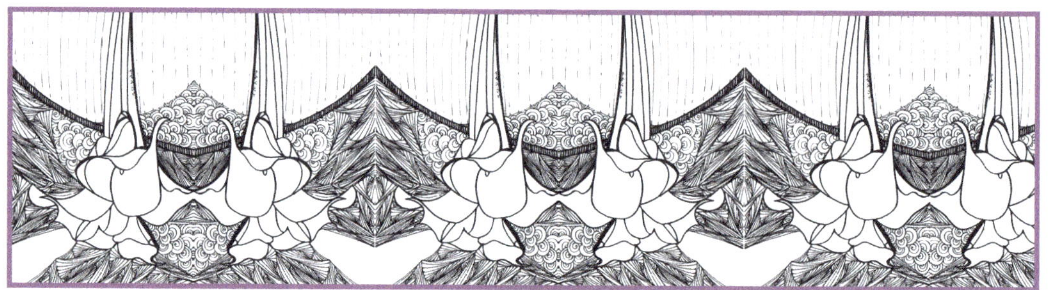

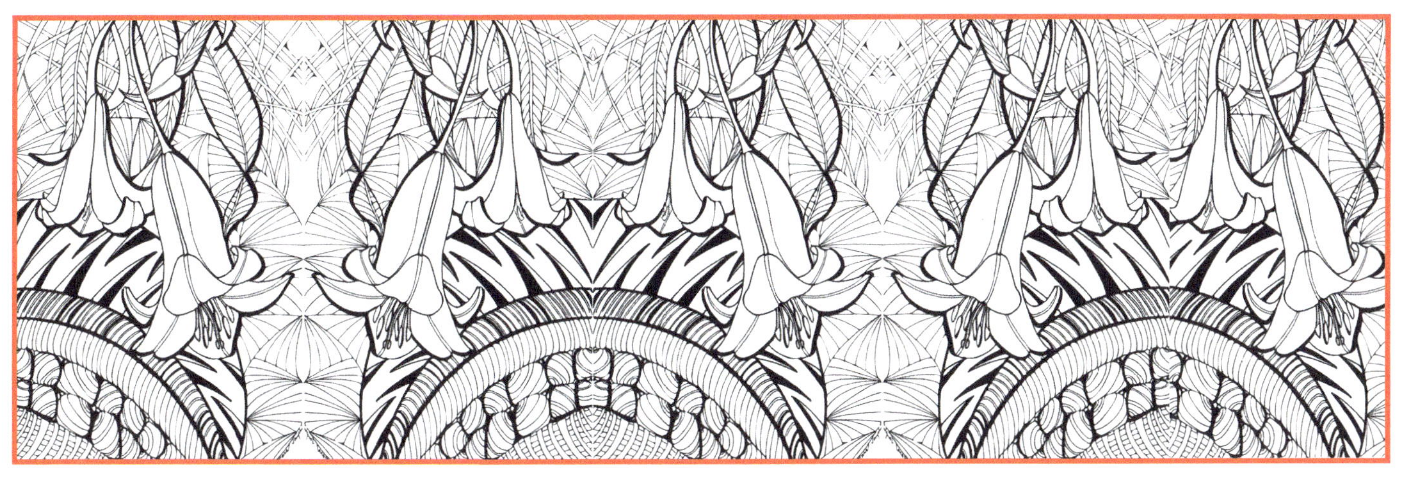

"Consider the lilies how they grow:

they toil not, they spin not;

and yet I say unto you,

that Solomon in all his glory was not arrayed like one of these.

If then God so clothe the grass,

which is today in the field, and tomorrow is cast into the oven;

how much more will he clothe you, O ye of little faith?

And seek not ye what ye shall eat, or what ye shall drink,

neither be ye of doubtful mind.

For all these things do the nations of the world seek after:

and your Father knoweth that ye have need of these things.

But rather seek ye the kingdom of God;

and all these things shall be added unto you.

Fear not, little flock; for it is your Father's good pleasure to give you
the kingdom."

Luke 12:27–32

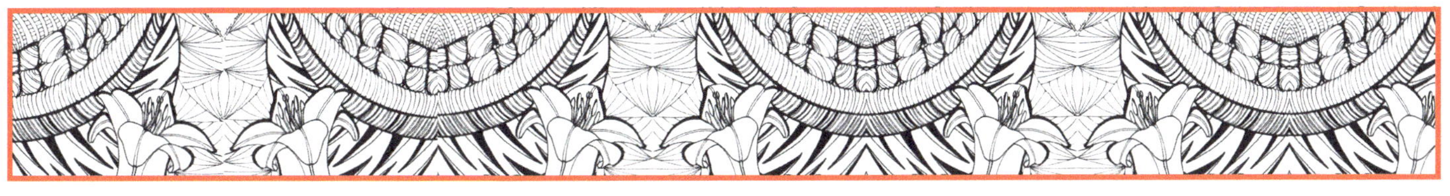

"Consider the Lilies How They Grow"

How do lilies grow? Dancing in the wind, with their glossy leaves of spear-shaped perfection—coddling fleshy stems and elegant blooms, they are a sight to behold! Jesus felt they deserved more than a casual glance of appreciation. He taught that there was insight to be gained by paying attention to them.

Think about this—cell by cell, invisible to our casual observation, the lily grows until one day we become captivated with its sculptural beauty. You too are growing. Change and maturation are assured. The lilies of the field do little to encourage their own growth. The sun warms them, the soil nurtures them, and they grow.

You do not have to know how growth happens. Lilies yield to the warm sun and timely showers. You too can simply submit to the process. Allow God's Word to be your source of refreshment and nourishment.

"As newborn babes, desire the sincere milk of the word, that ye may grow thereby." 1 Peter 2:2

Do you have a burning desire for God's Word? If not, ask Him for the passion that will feed and strengthen your spirit, because when you are nourished by His Word, every aspect of your life will surely be transformed.

Read it, write it, memorize it, and think upon it. Ask for wisdom and new insight about it. Dialogue with God about it.

Never treat verses with familiarity, because the riches of God's Word cannot be mined in one, or even many, lifetimes!

Growth of the sort that you desire will happen at first without you perceiving it. Eventually it will become apparent to you and then to others.

Your life too, like the lily, will have its moment of breathtaking perfection when in full bloom it will command attention.

"Night and day, whether he sleeps or gets up, the seed sprouts and grows,
though he does not know how." Mark 4:2

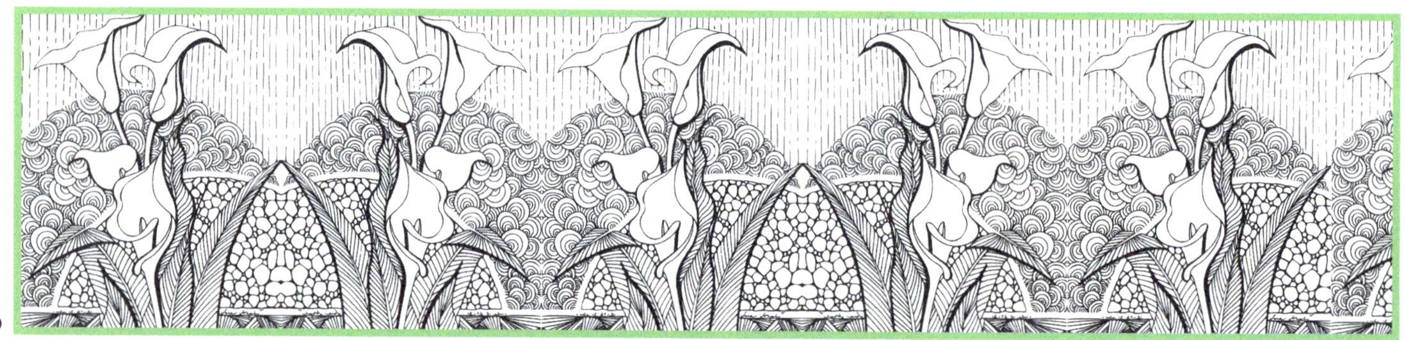

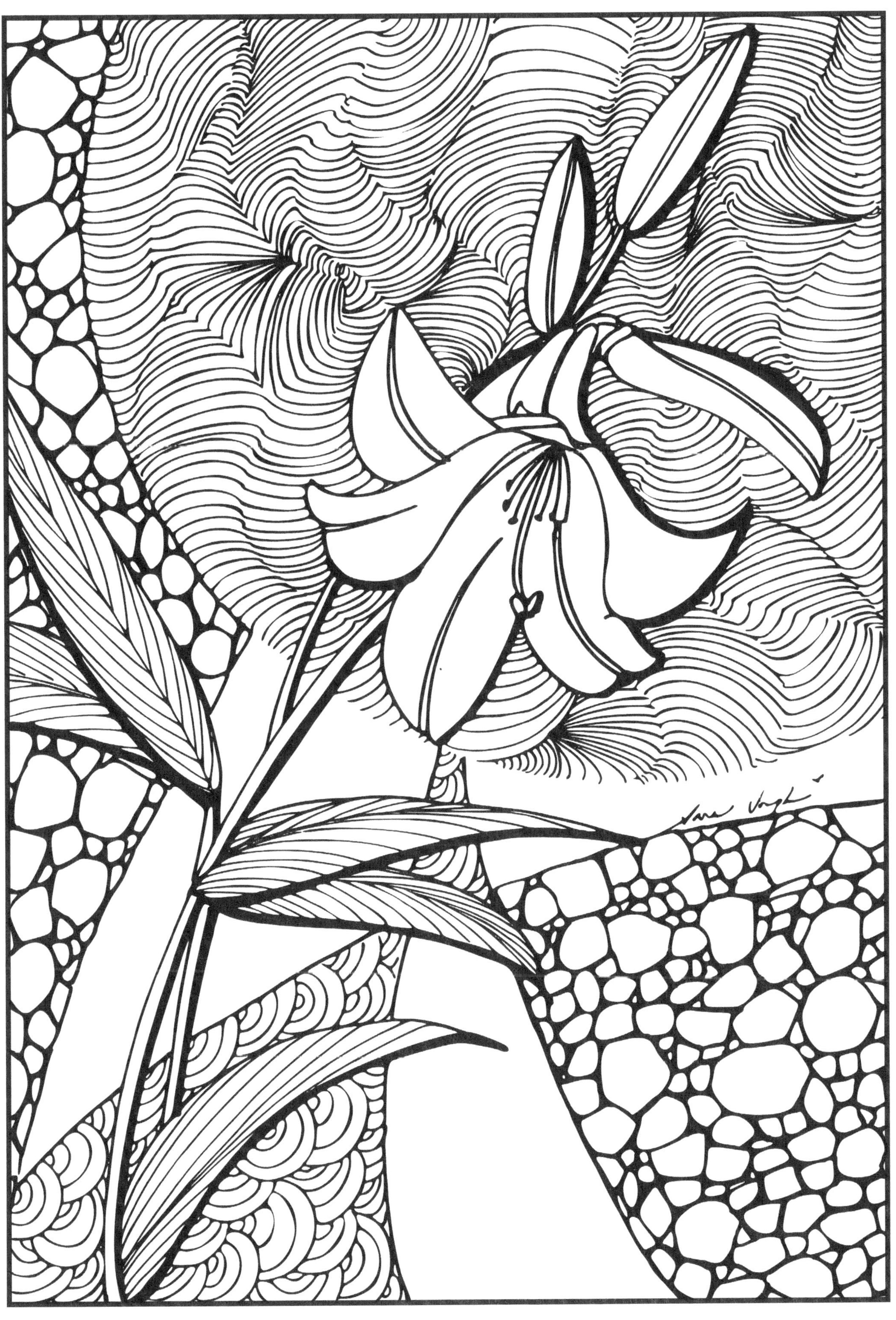

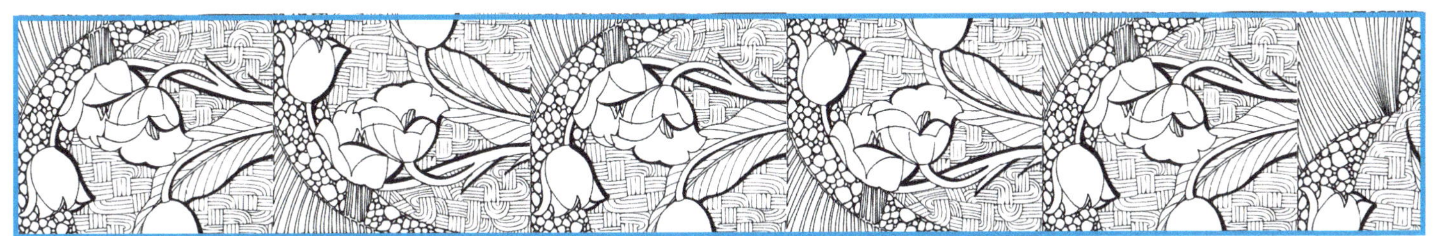

How Have You Grown Lately?

Thank God for the changes the Lord has already wrought in you. The very act of acknowledging growth will empower you with the expectation of more. Record how different you are now from who you once were. Enter it here as a tangible record for the future. Describe whatever progress you perceive, regardless of how small it may seem. One day you will look back on these pages and smile with gratitude. Purpose to continually allow the Word and the Holy Spirit to conform you into the image of Jesus, the Author and Perfecter of your faith.

*"As thou knowest not
what is the way of the spirit,
nor how the bones do grow
in the womb of her
that is with child:
even so thou knowest not
the works of God
who maketh all."*
Ecclesiastes 11:5

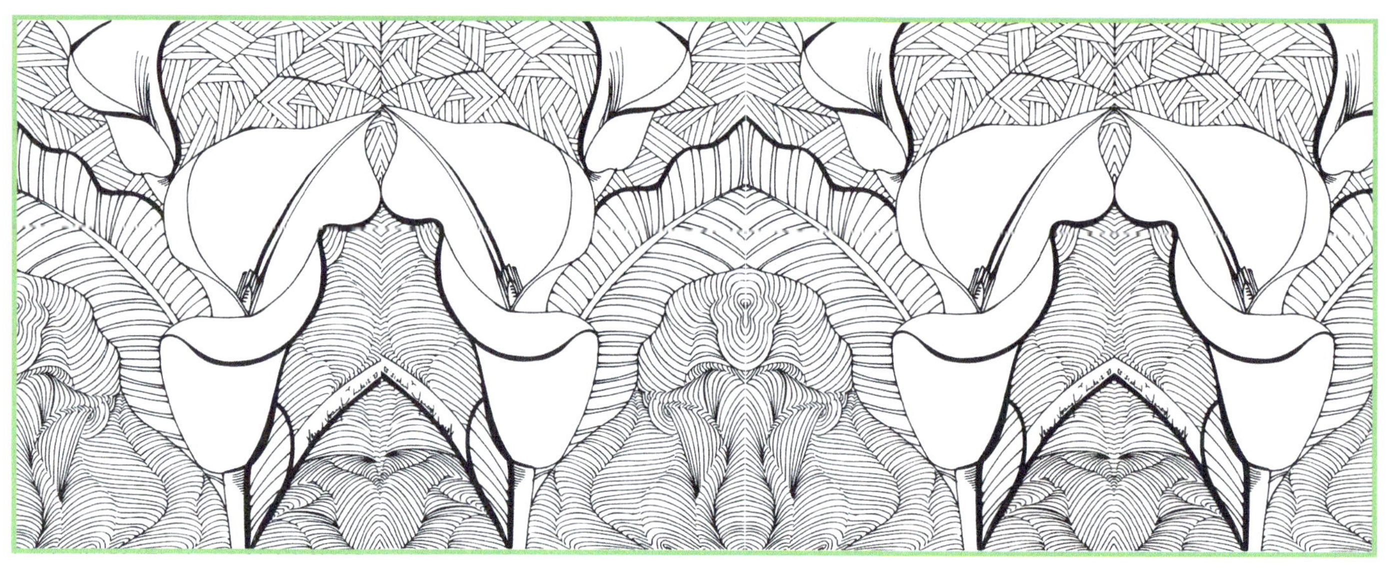

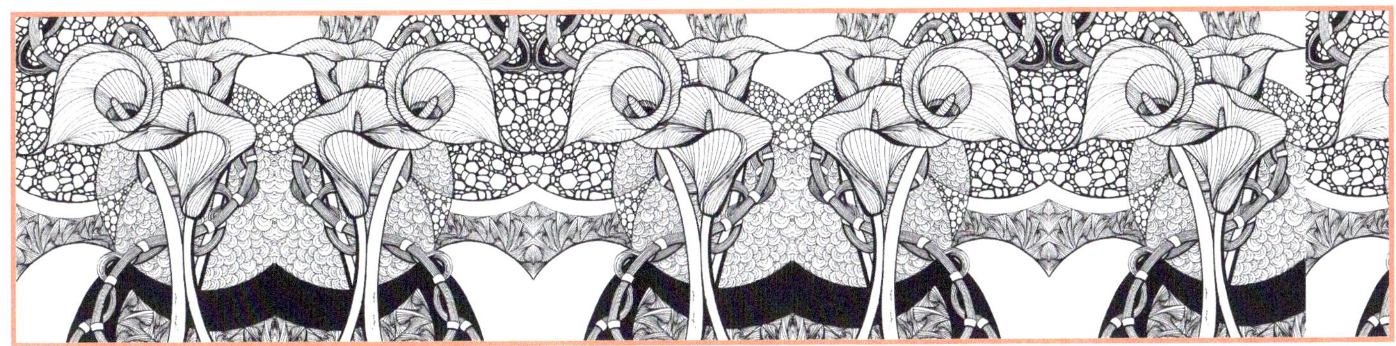

GROWTH

Are you yearning for growth but unable to see it at the moment? God promises to work in you if you surrender. Trust that what He has promised He will fulfill.

Describe changes that you would like to see in your life. Fill the next pages with these secrets of your heart. Entrust them to God. Dream, aspire, and imagine. Don't limit yourself by what you think is possible. It is God's responsibility to work in you. Allow Him to paint a vision of your future. His plans are always thrilling and better than anything we could ever imagine.

How gracious He is, and how marvelous is His working in a yielded heart!

"For it is God who works in you, to will and to act, in order to fulfill his good purpose."
Philippians 2:13

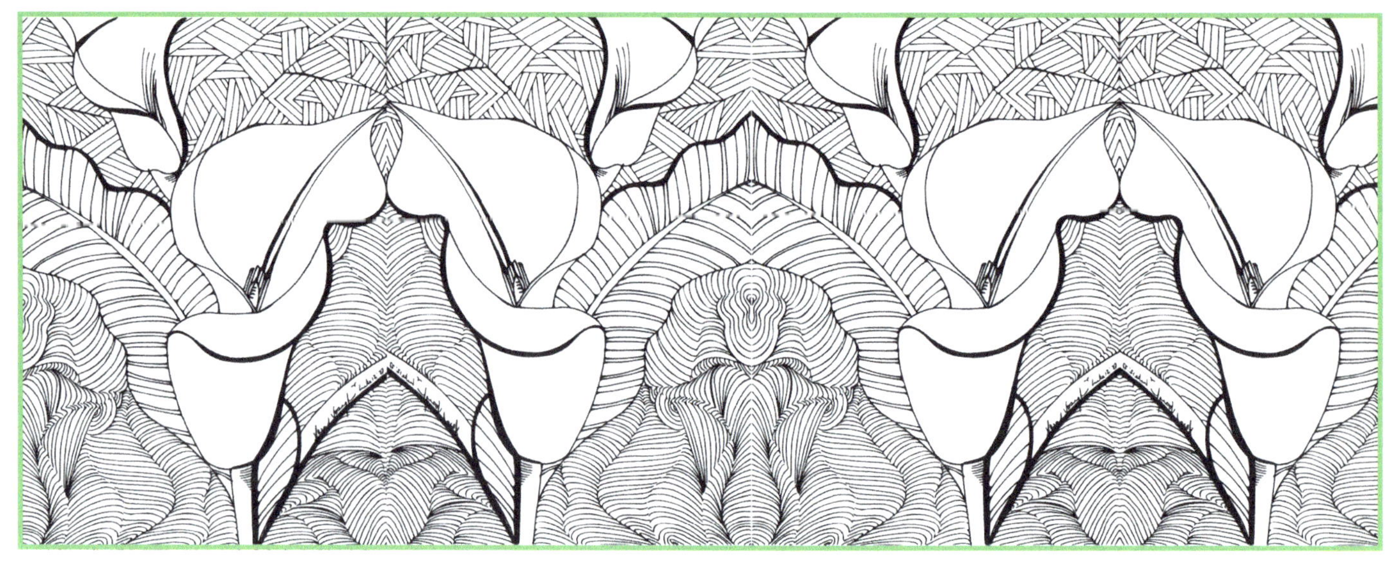

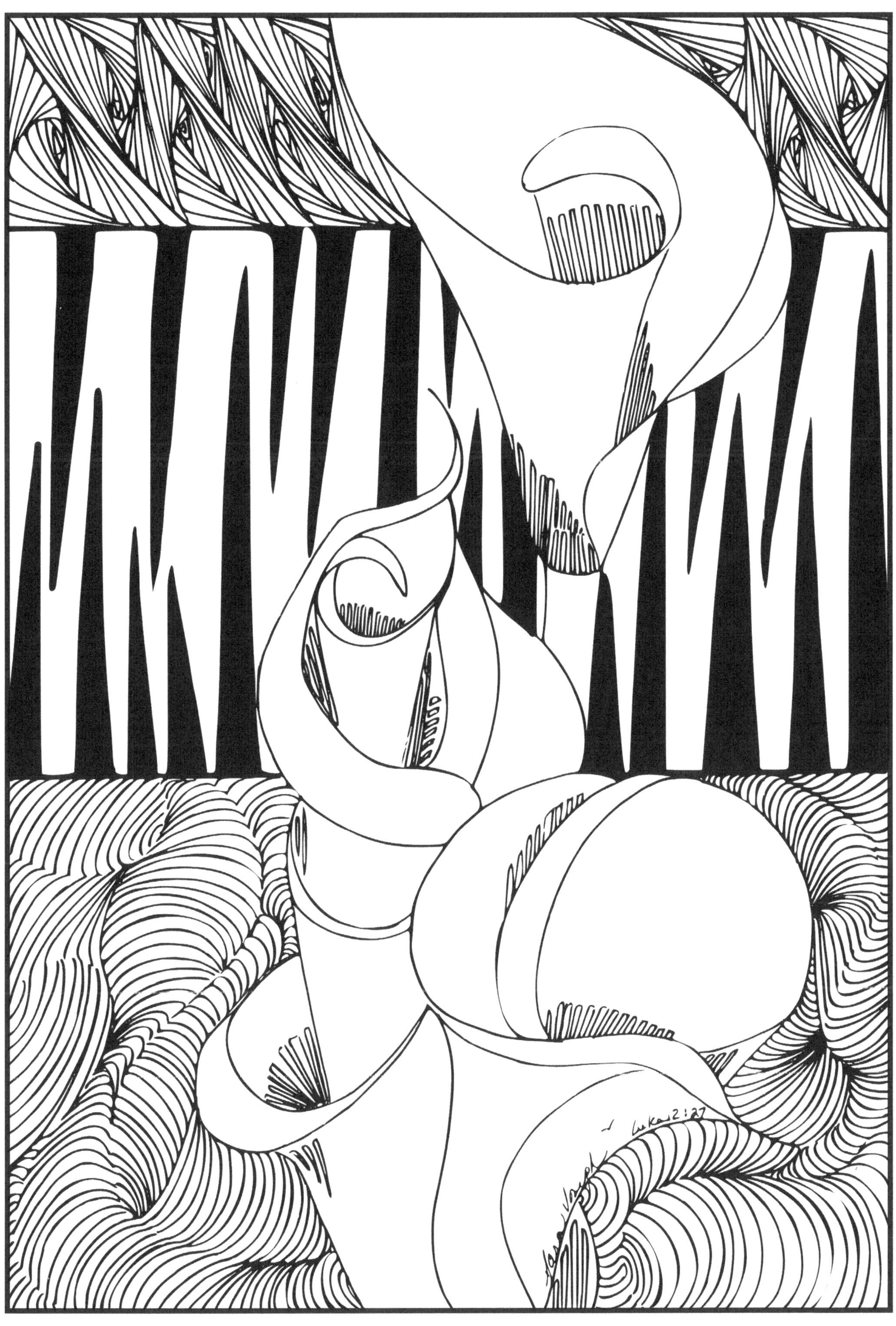

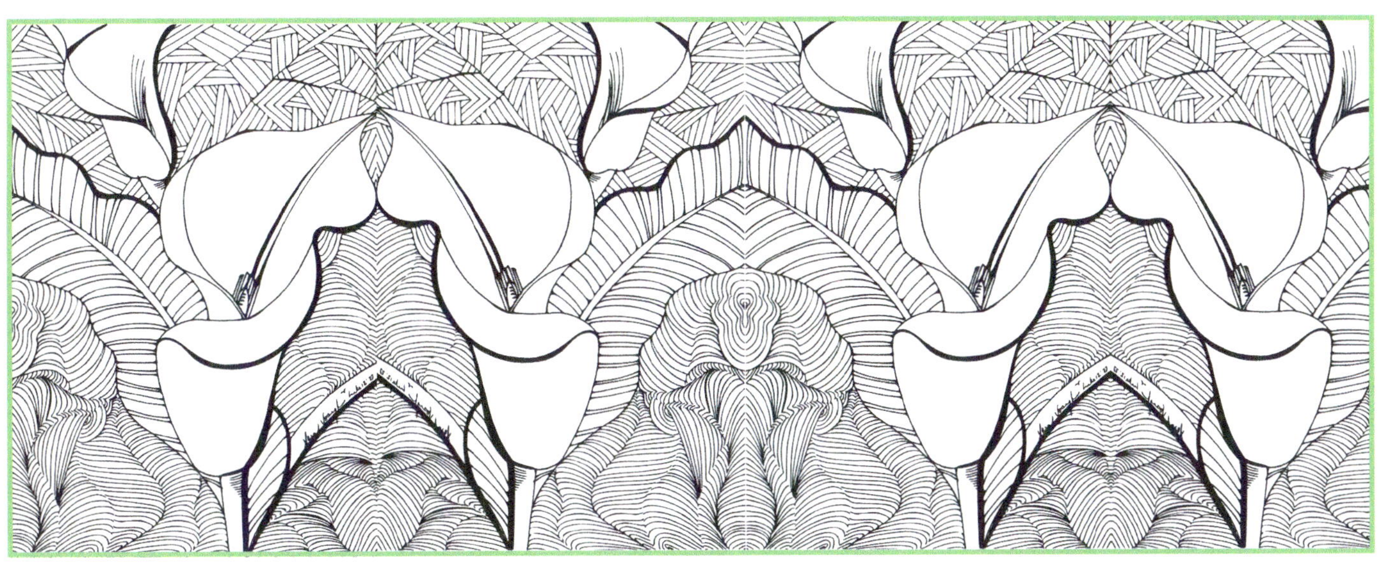

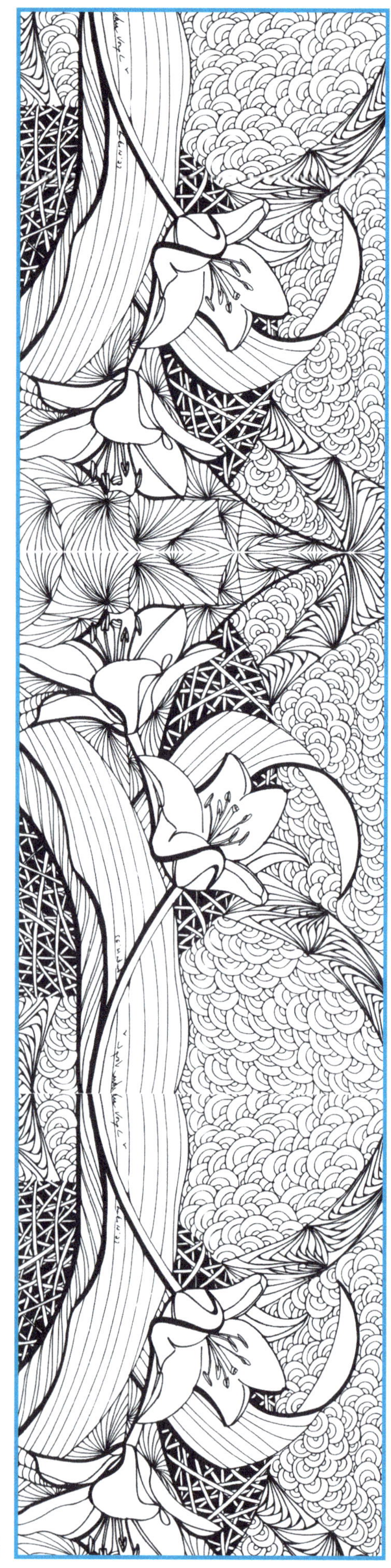

Toil Not

May your life lived in Christ
Brim over with excess
Not vain, ceaseless labor,
For God promises to bless

May His favor so cling
To your time here on earth
That your days may be thrilling
With bounty unearthed

Pleasing then will your life surely be
Happy and full with fruit that abounds
For toil depletes, is hopeless and dreary
Toil not then, but in Him be found

Oh, may dull sapping labor
Be the embers of your past
While outrageous favor
You will never outlast

Freedom from toil seems surely absurd
Preposterous, yet it is God's Word
Carefree to thrive as the lily fair
Swaying with ease in the summer air

Consider the lily
That strove not for its grace
But solely to His light
Did turn its pure face

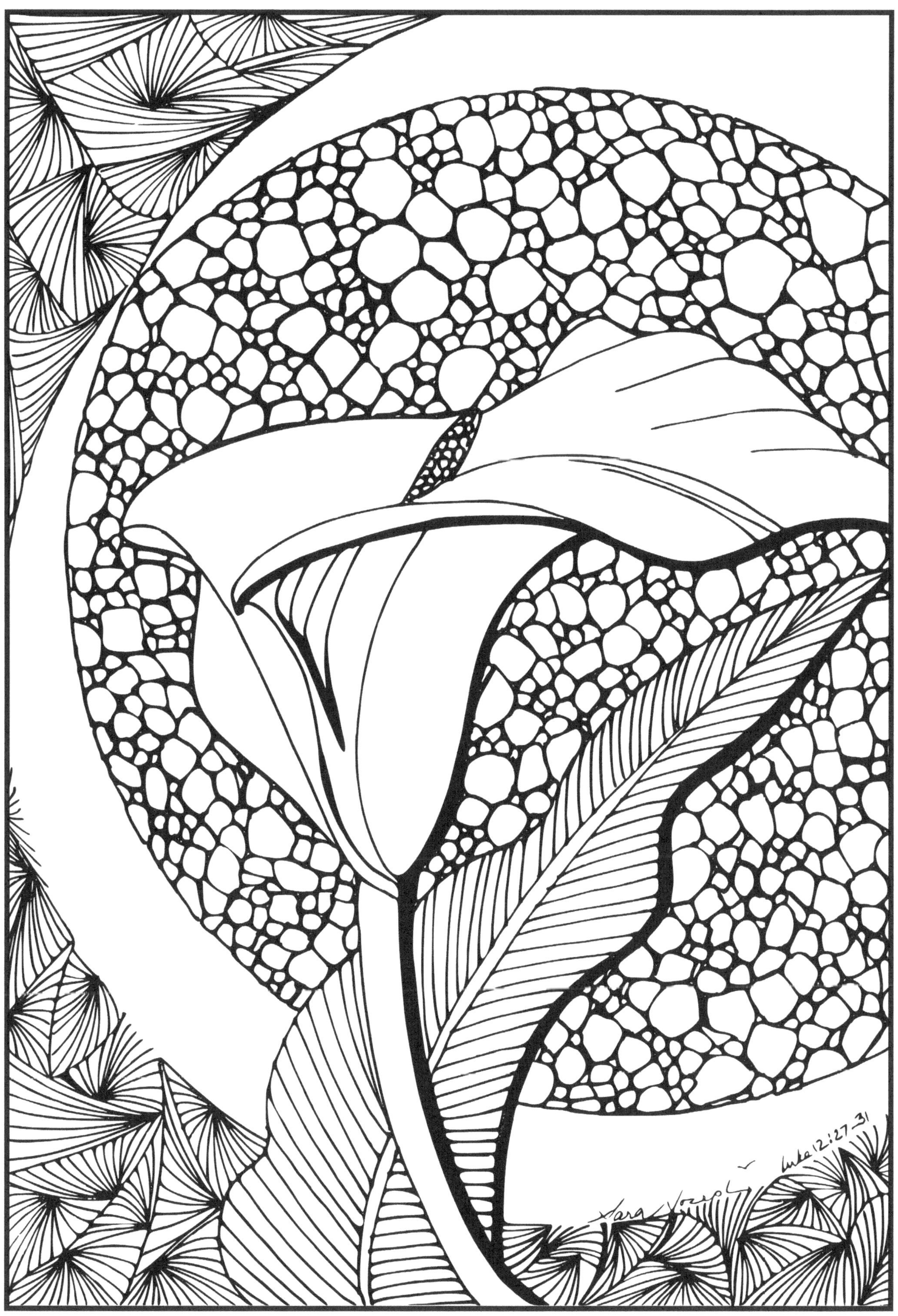

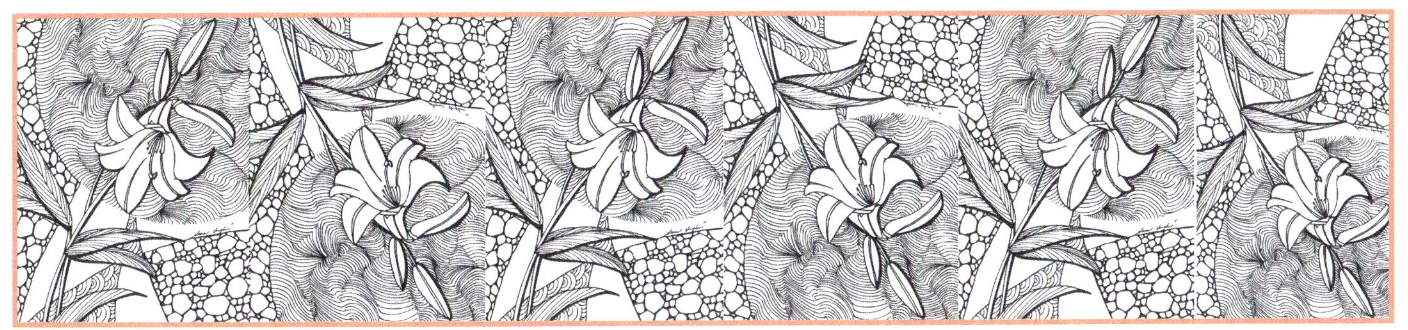

The Blessed Life

In all its pristine glory, the lily does not labor but depends on the Creator for dew and sunshine, for beauty and grace. You can too.

Is your life a continual struggle? Then you are not living the abundant life as God intended. Yes, some seasons will seem bleak. But those will pass if you trust God. You can learn from the Bible how to receive His blessing, which is conditional. Gladly obey all His commands; His rewards for a surrendered life are more than worth it! Take some time to read Deuteronomy 28:1-14, and let the promises percolate in your spirit.

What are your thoughts about a blessing that is so complete, so abundant, and so excellent? This is God's will for you. Read these verses mindful that this is a contract between God and you. Put your name on it, expect it, watch for it, and yield to it continually.

"The blessing of the Lord, it maketh rich, and He addeth no sorrow with it." Proverbs 10:22

How will you exchange your toil for the joy of living in the blessing? The difference between the two is so vast that if you do not understand it, you must ask God for insight. Spend time thinking about the contrast between hopelessly struggling and enjoying the blessing. Explore it in words. Grasping this difference will truly change your life.

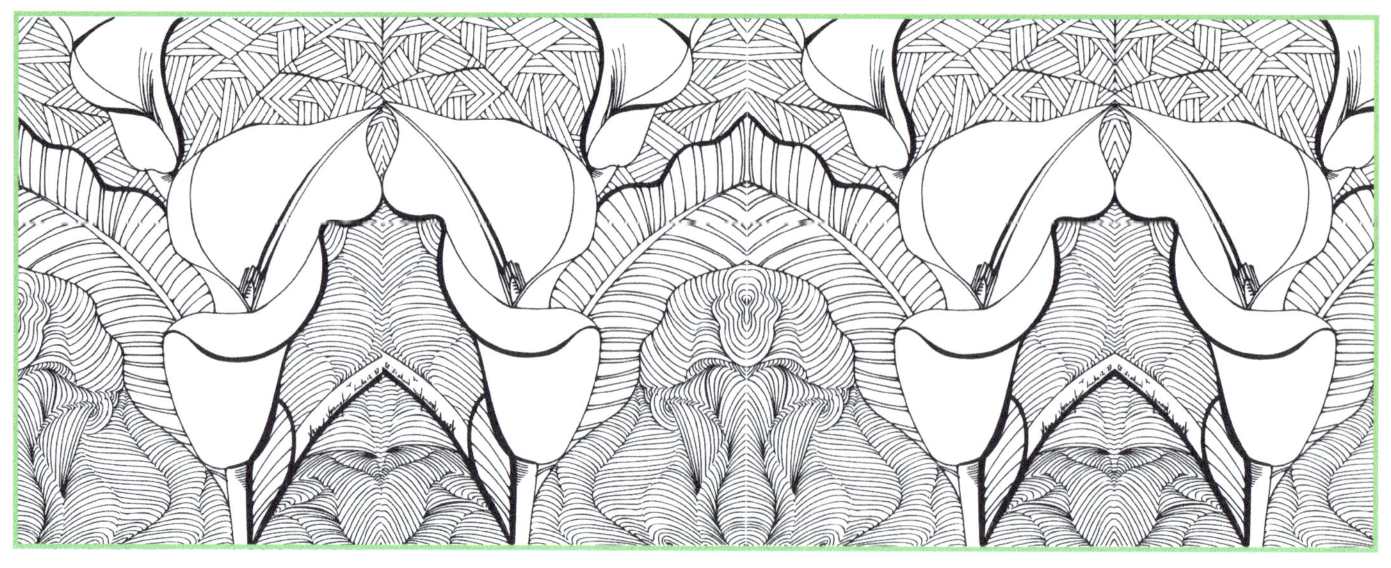

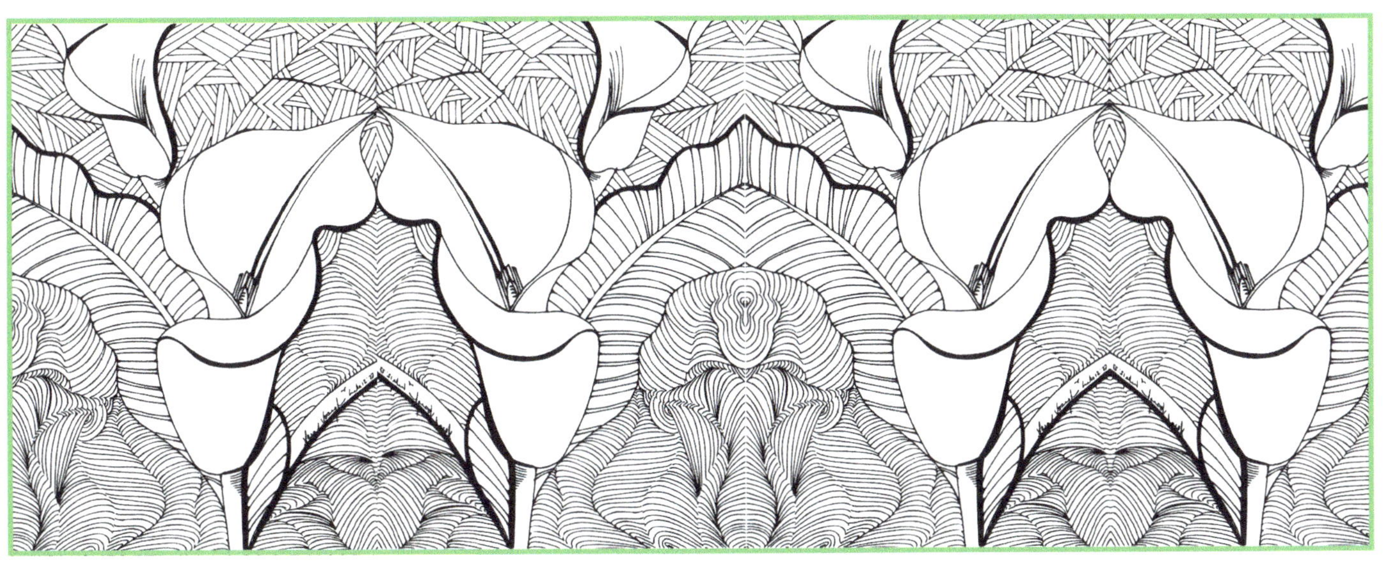

What one struggle can you turn over today, trusting God to provide and care for you? Write down your most pressing concern—not to dwell on it, but to turn it over to God. Release it and refuse to be burdened with it anymore! Date this, because one day you will want to look back with delight to see how marvelously God handled this very issue.

____

____

____

____

____

____

____

____

____

____

____

Is God's Spirit prompting some action on your part as you trust Him with your concern? God usually encourages a little step of faith in response to His promises. Write it down and obey.

____

____

____

____

____

____

____

____

How will you work hard but keep yourself from toiling in vain? God will entrust you with work to be accomplished in His kingdom, but there is nothing burdensome about it. Ask Him for His marching orders, knowing that you will surely face challenges. We live in a fallen world, and we are not exempt from its taint. But don't worry; His provision will be more than adequate if you step out in faith.

____

____

____

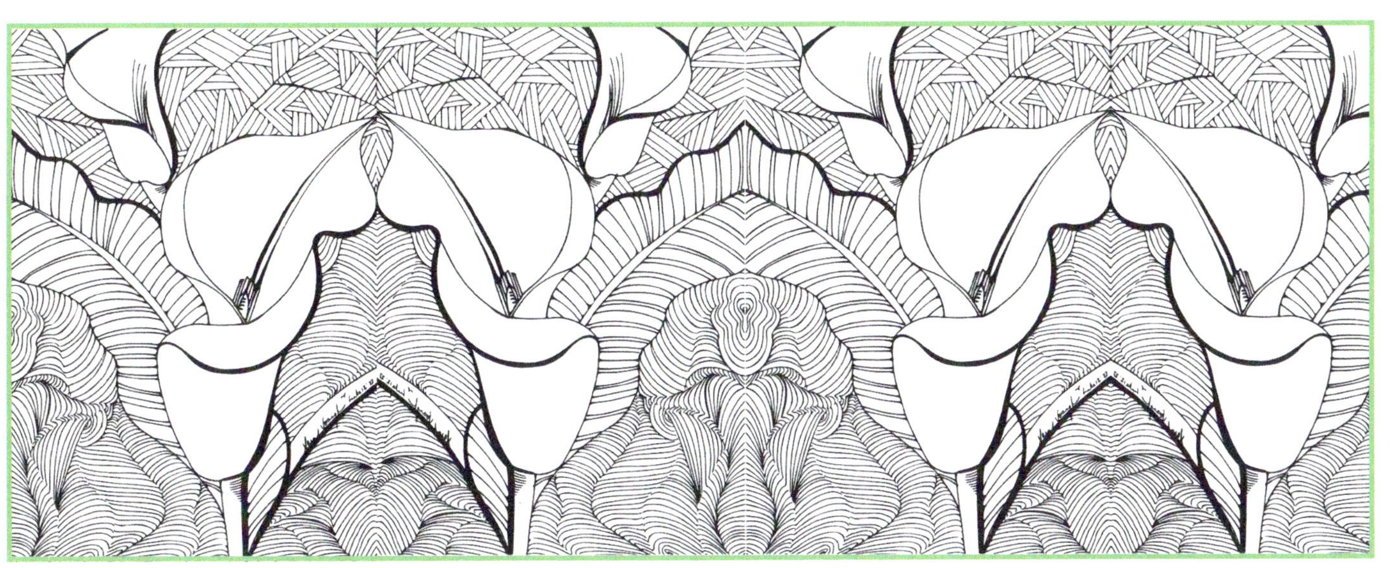

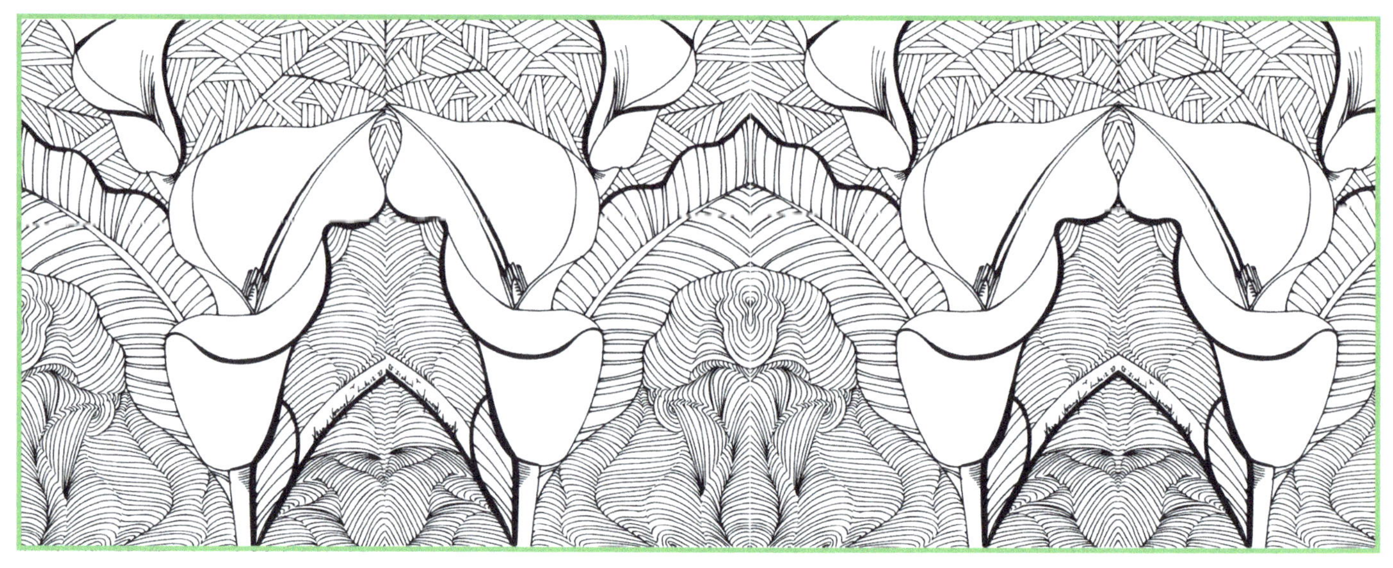

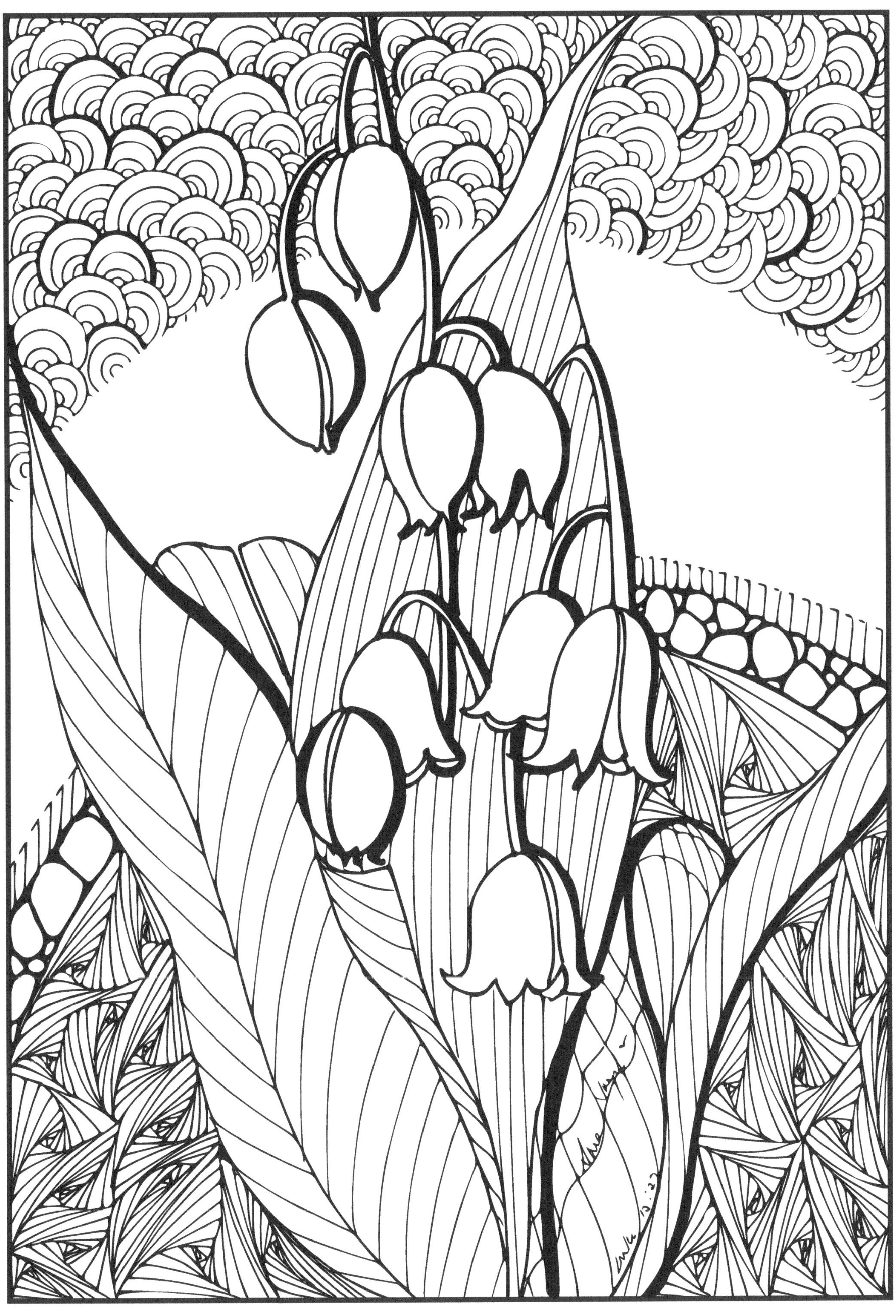

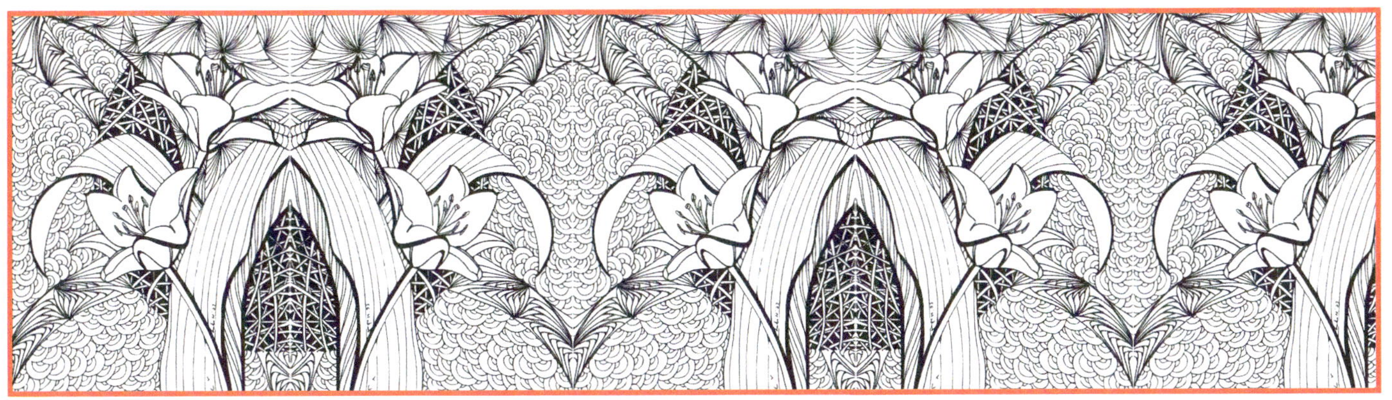

Drawing Closer

There is a subtle, but significant, difference between strenuous stress-free labor at tasks God has called you to and toiling at something of your own choosing. Who is in charge of your day? Who has chosen your tasks? Consider all that consumes your time. Switch taskmasters if you tend to make wrong choices by listening to wrong voices.

"Draw nigh to God, and He will draw nigh to you.

Cleanse your hands, ye sinners; and purify your hearts, ye double minded." James 4:8

Make no room in your life for sin or a lack of faith. Both will undermine your growth. Ask for forgiveness for sins He brings to mind. Receive the forgiveness He promises and press on. Determine to believe every promise that you read in the Bible, regardless of how improbable its fulfillment may seem at the moment. That is faith, which pleases God.

The invitation to "Consider the lily" is Jesus beckoning you to a different sort of living. You can live a joyous life that is of His making, not birthed out of your striving!

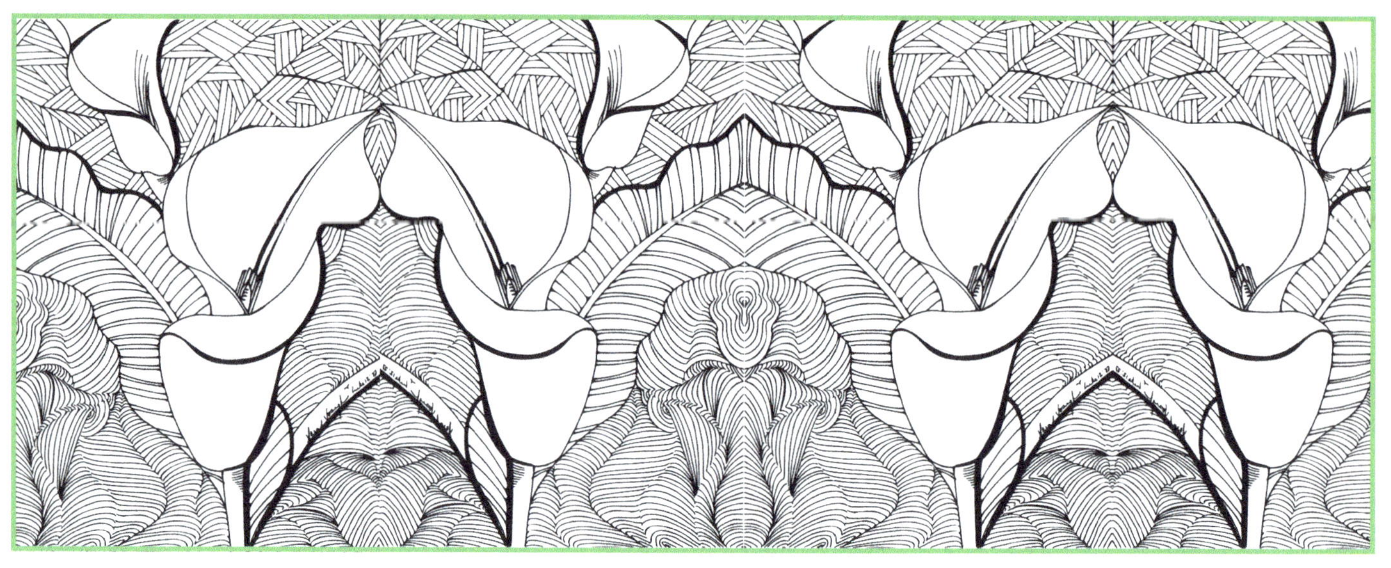

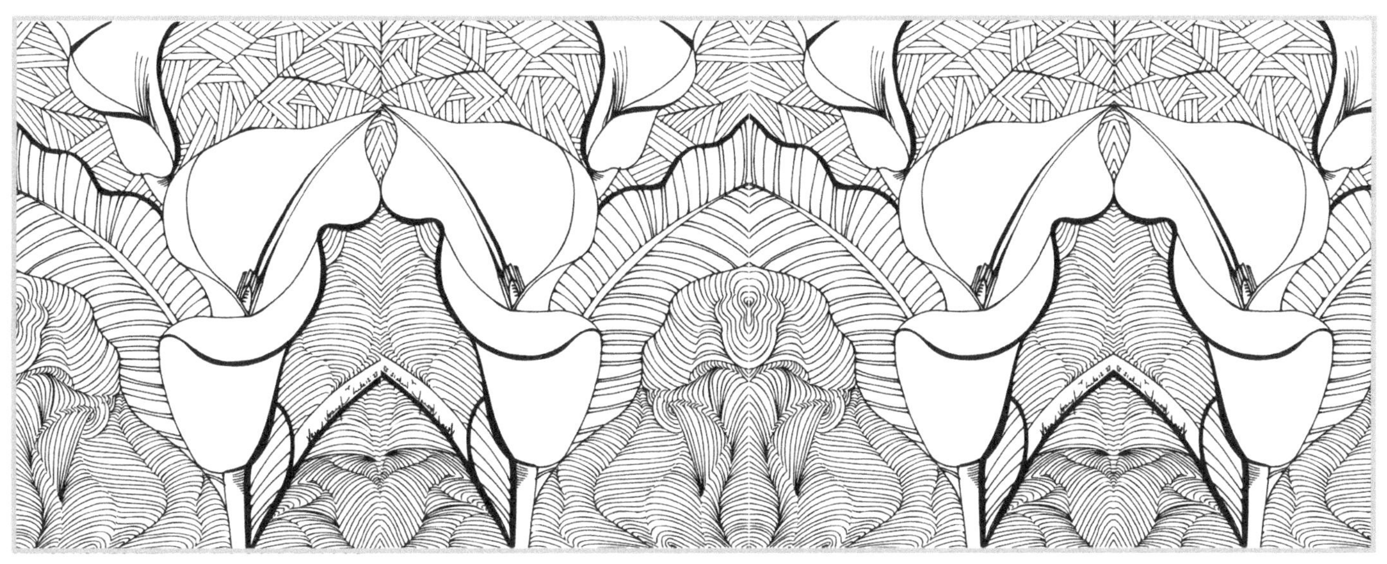

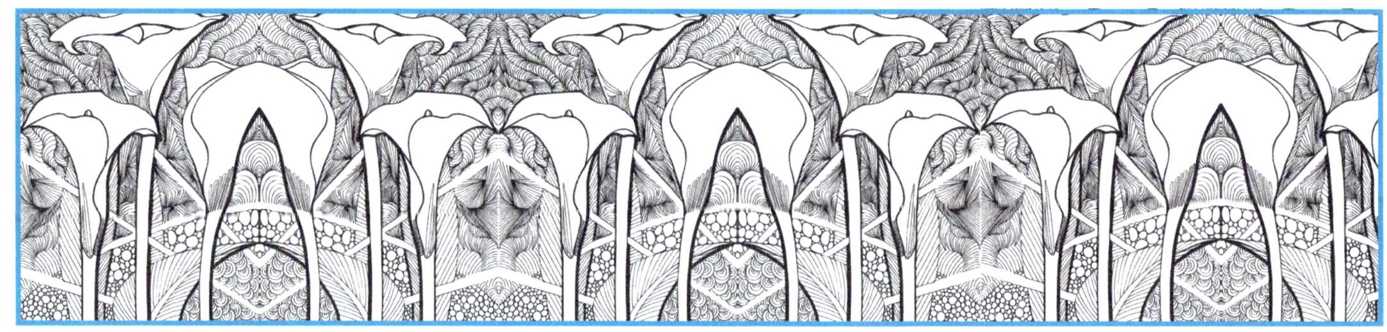

A Time to Pray

If life is a struggle and you see no way around your present challenges, take time to pray as you color. He will give you the awareness you seek. He holds all the answers, so trust Him to reveal them to you.

Journal your thoughts on this page as a conversation between God and you. Prayer is both your words to Him and your listening for His response. The whisper of His voice can easily be missed if you do not still yourself. Write down what you hear. If you have never done this before and are uncomfortable, relax. When you demonstrate an eagerness to hear from God, He promises to grace you with His presence. Just remember to be honest before Him. Steadfastly choose to believe Him when He speaks.

If you are convinced God never speaks to you, pick up your Bible and begin reading anywhere. Listen. He is speaking. What words from the Bible apply to your situation?

Unable to find anything? Keep reading until you do. There are so many great and precious promises that you won't have to read too much before you find one that will put a smile on your face and a spring in your step.

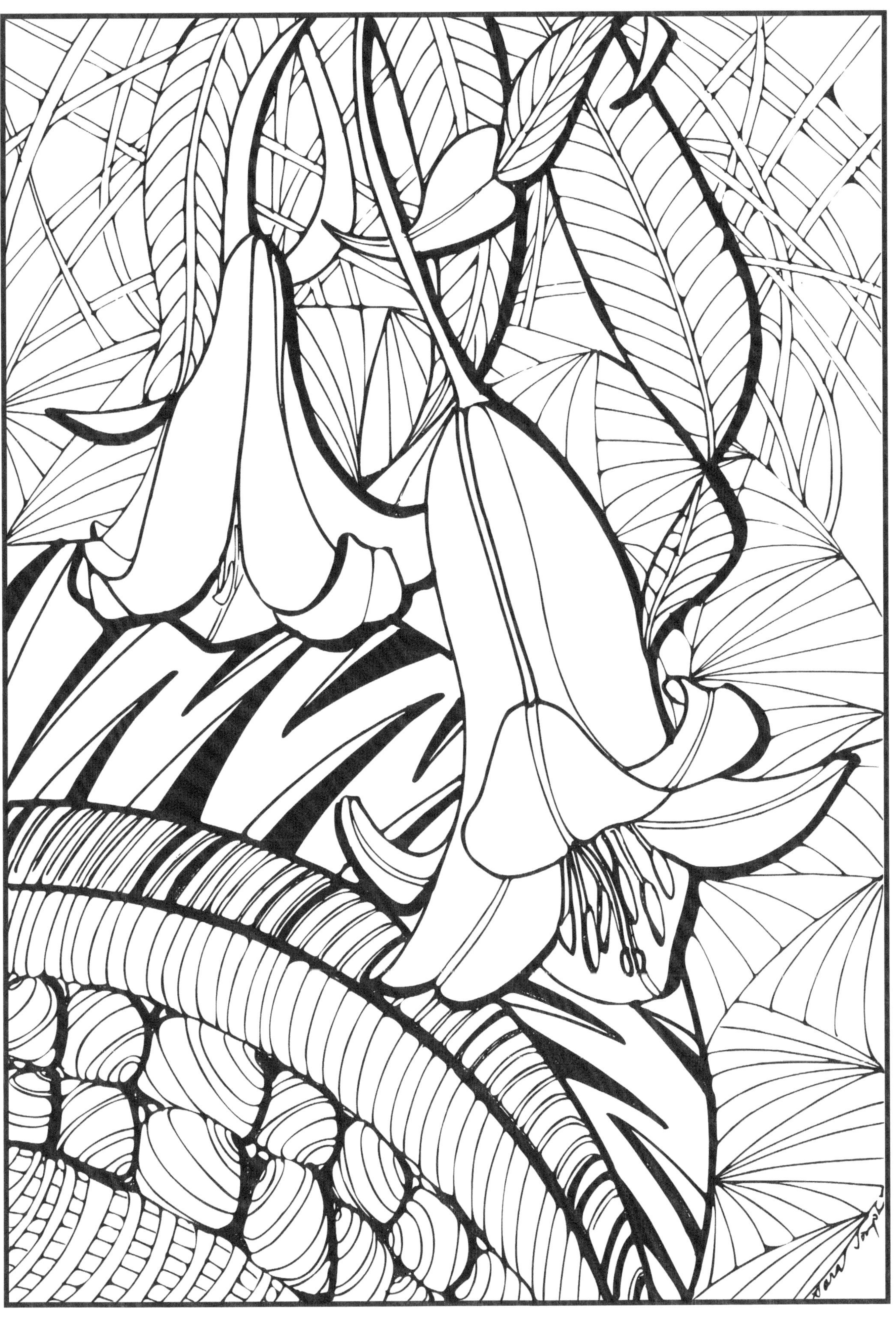

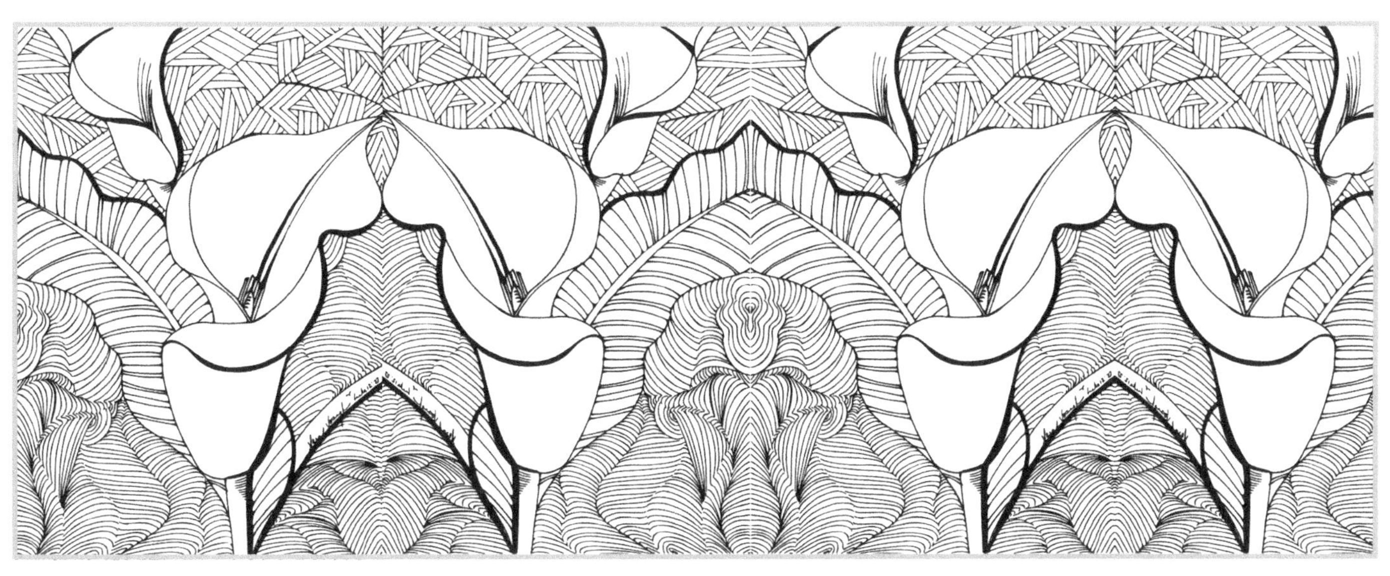

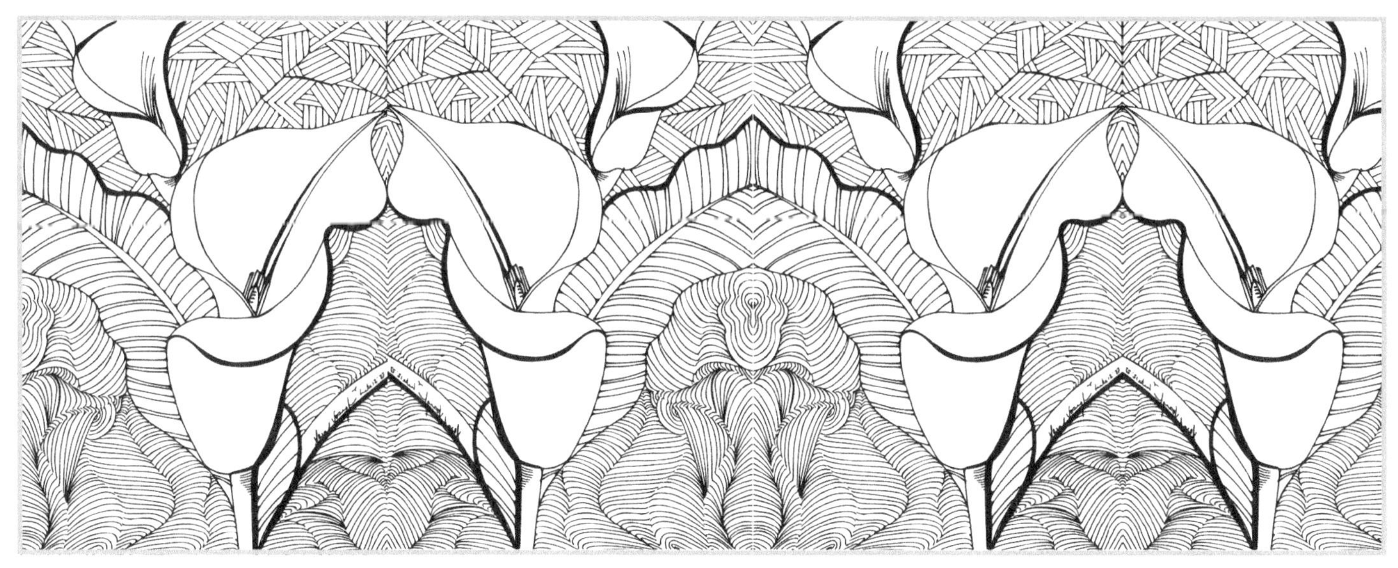

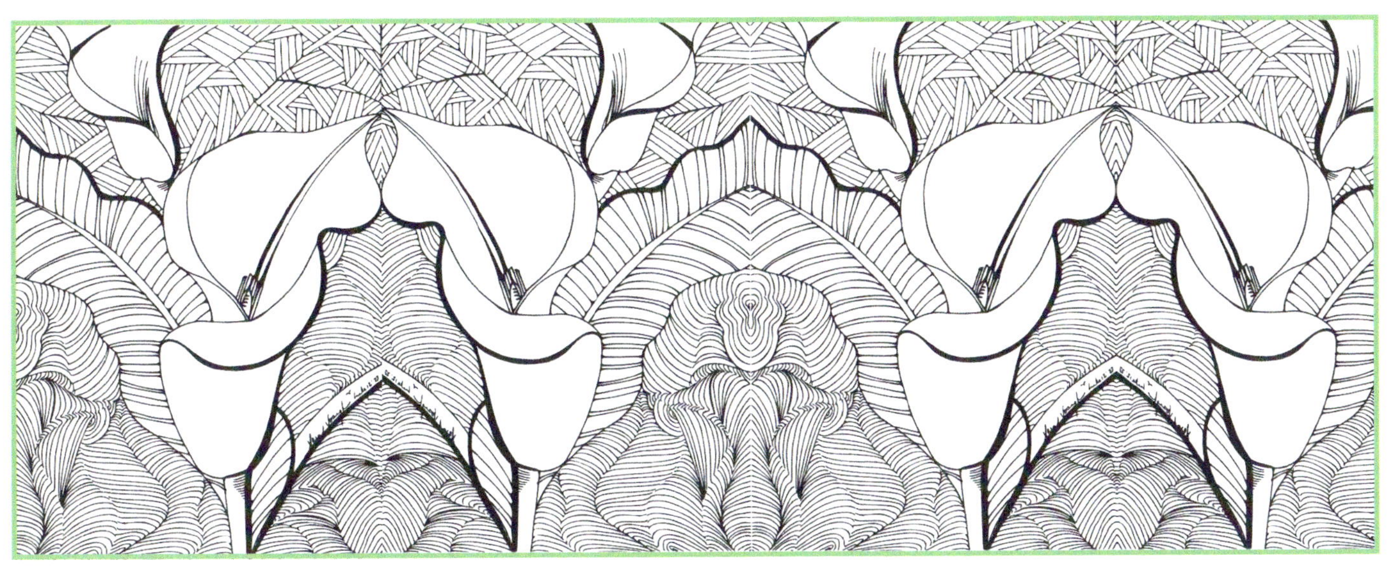

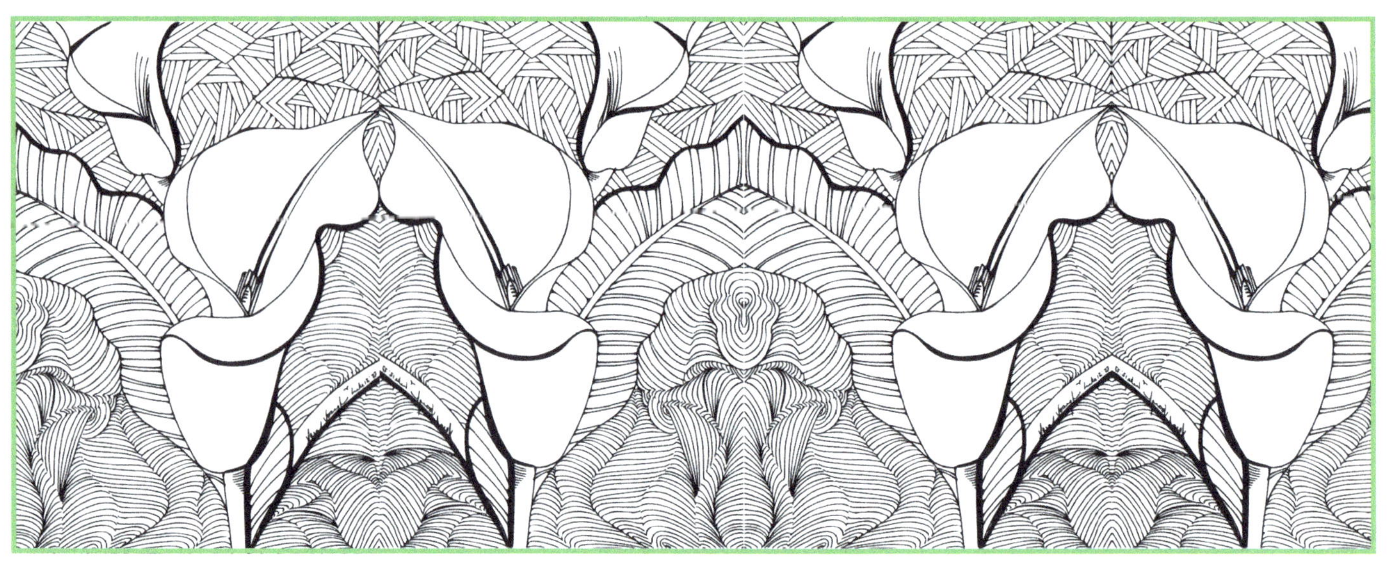

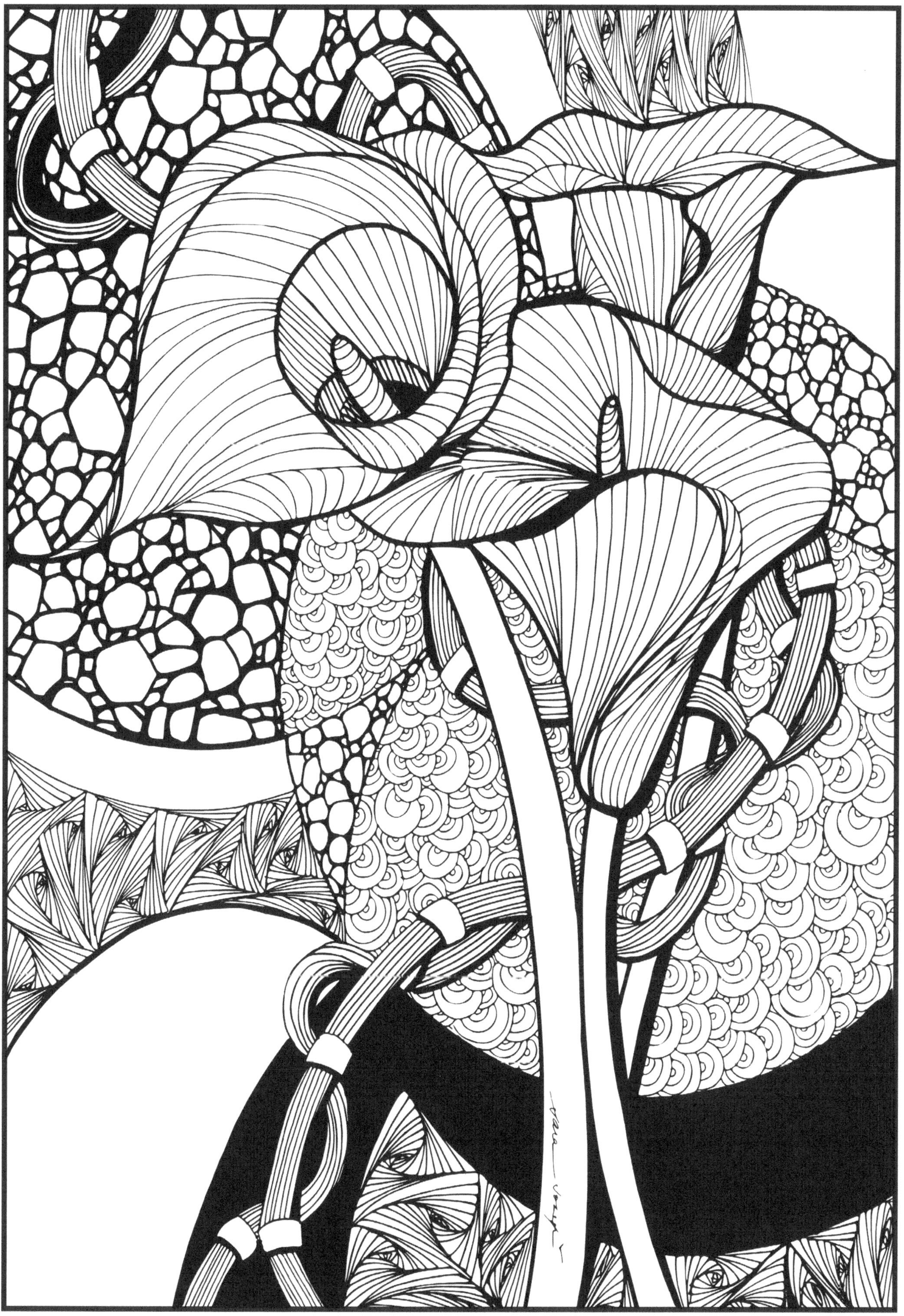

"Consider the lilies how they grow: they toil not, they spin not;
and yet I say unto you,
that Solomon in all his glory was not arrayed like one of these." Luke 12:27

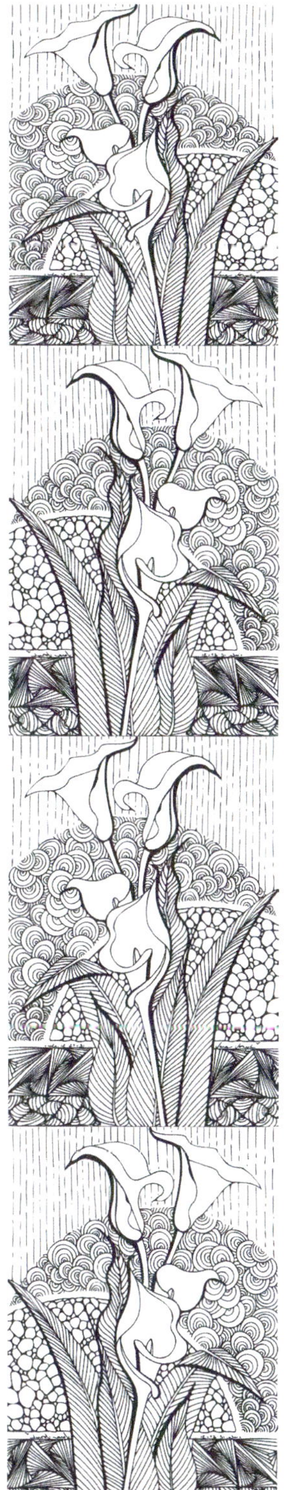

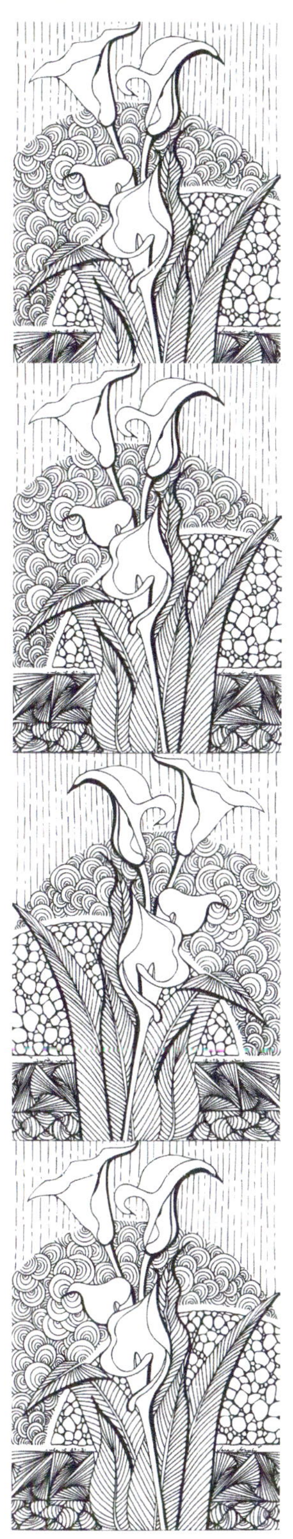

The Lily

Yellow and dazzling, gold was aplenty
Goblets and lamps, a throne of pale ivory
Sleek and burnished, gold gobbled the light
Bouncing off lions' manes, tawny and bright

Cinnamon and saffron, pepper and cloves
Choice meat swimming in sauces with loaves
Fragrantly bountiful from oven to table
Solomon's feasts were no ancient fable

Silver was common, rubies galore
Sapphires and diamonds, brocades a bore
Stallions, Arabians, and thoroughbreds too
Muscled and quivering to race forth on cue

Aromas of incense perfumed the air
Cedar and spices, and offerings of prayer
The grandeur of Solomon rendered speechless
A queen from abroad bearing great riches

More splendid by far is the lily in season
Than silks of Sheba or robes of Solomon
No artful spinning wove such brilliance
God alone made its milk-throated elegance

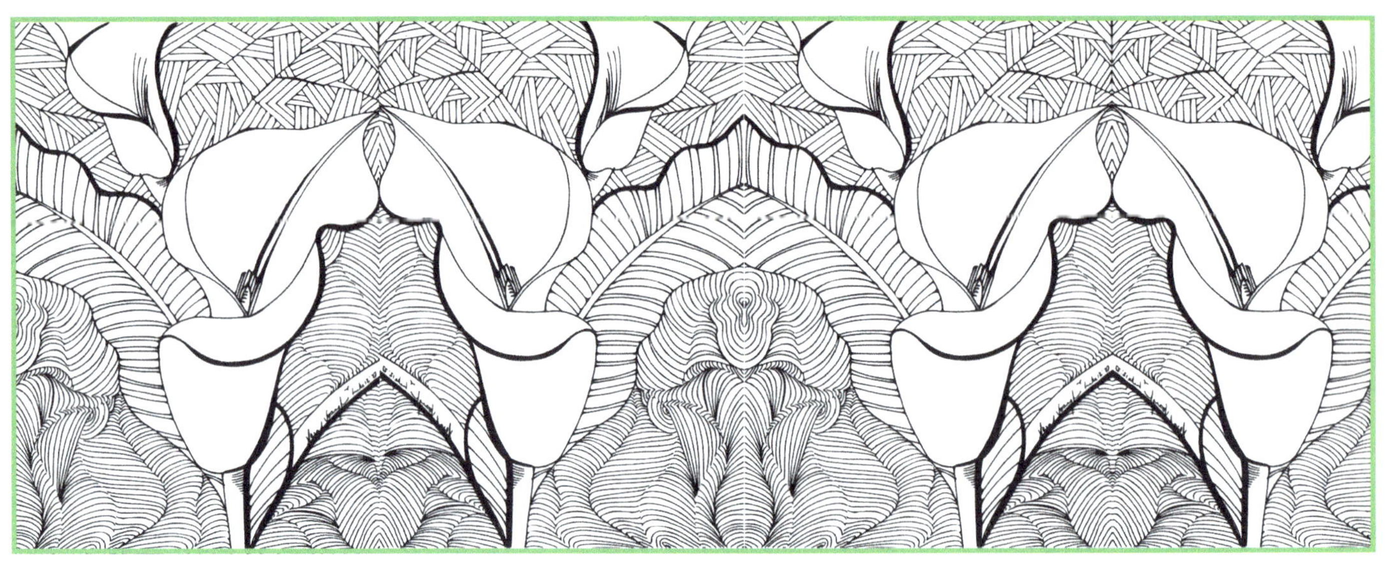

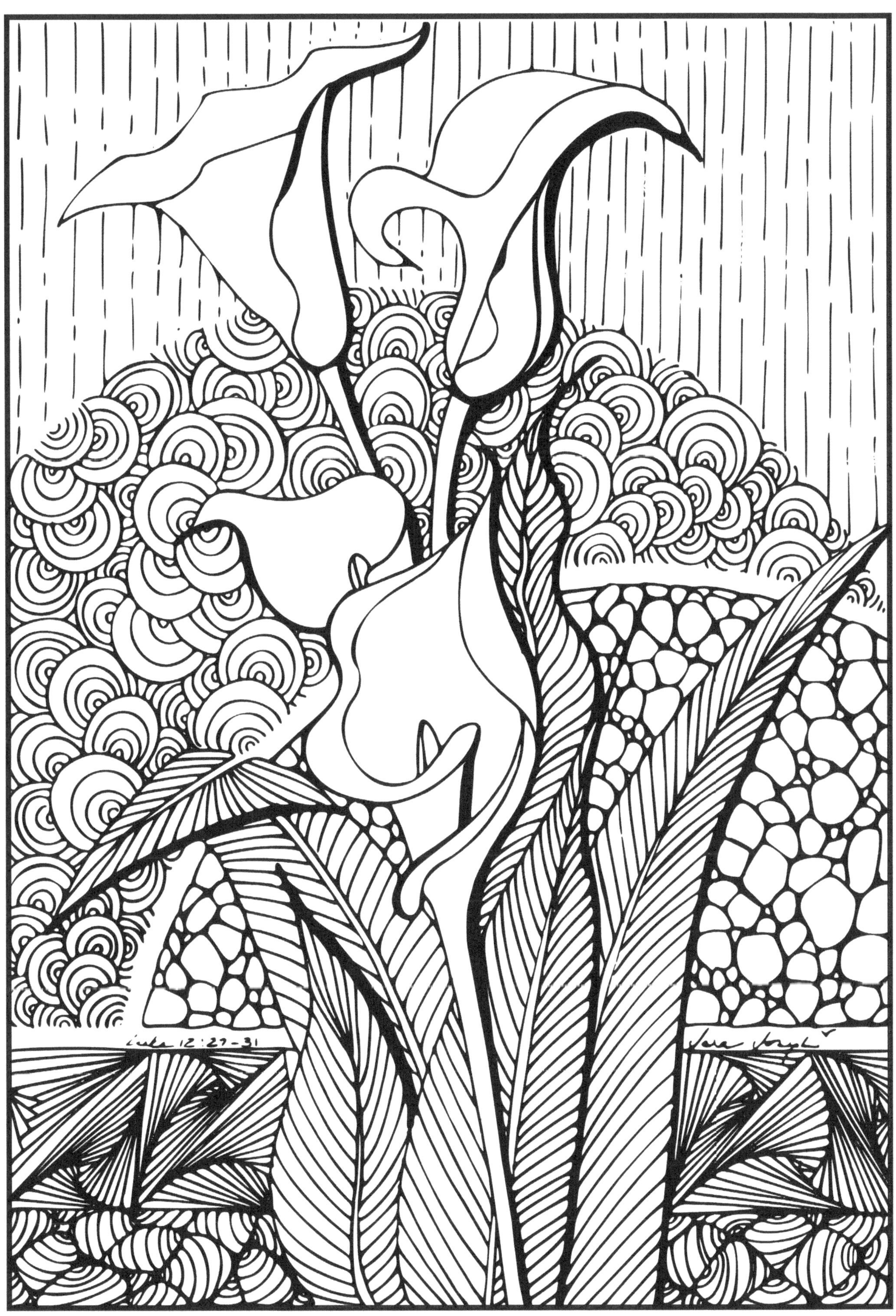

Luke 12:27-31

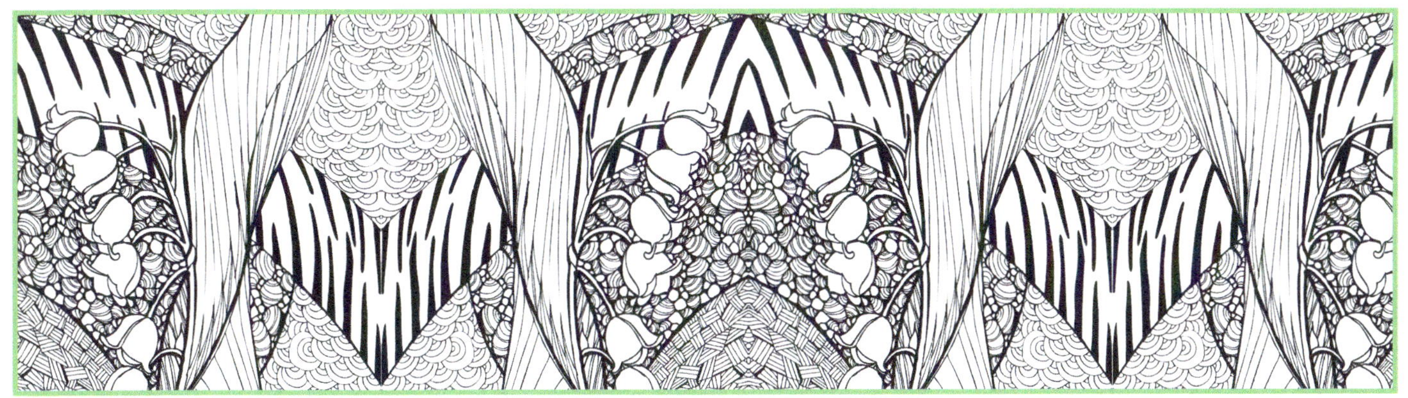

TRUE RICHES

We are awed by wealth. The more ostentatious its display, the more it beguiles us. Solomon's wealth took the queen of Sheba's breath away. Yet Jesus presents a different perspective of extravagant wealth by pointing to the lily.

Gloriously created, cared for, and sustained by the Father, the lily demonstrates what it means to be truly wealthy.

Can you dare believe Him today for such perfect care? Imagine your future if you lived as though you were assured of the Father's unfailing love. Why waste another moment worrying about anything when you could just take it to Him in prayer? Remind yourself of the lily turning her cup to be filled with the warmth of the sun and purpose to be the same way—dependent only on God for all your needs, wants, and desires.

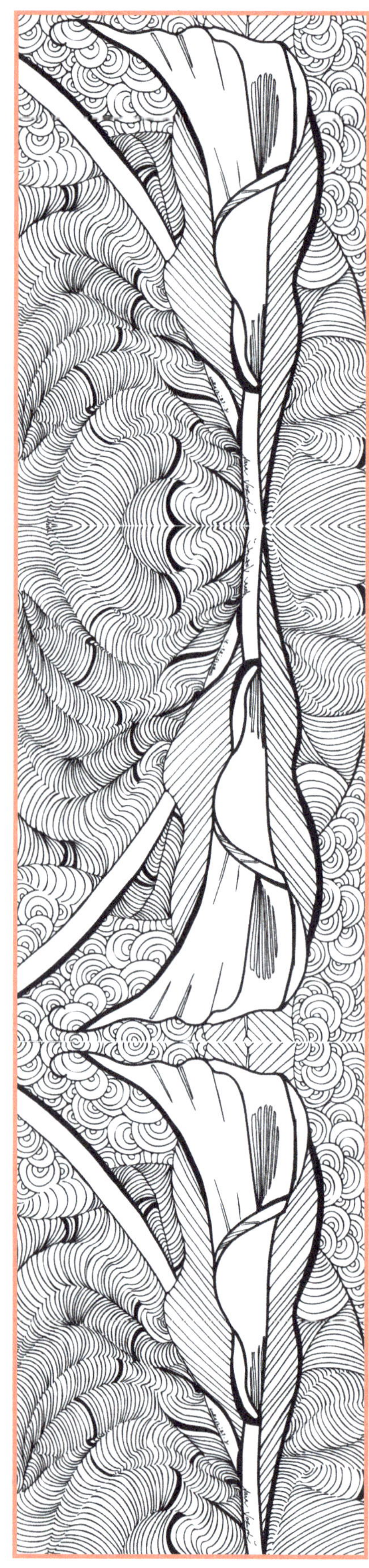

HOW MUCH MORE?

Why worry when He often tells me
No threat so great that I can foresee
Wields dark power over His love
To cause such harm I can't rise above?

Why cry for lack of urgent supply
When a prayer in faith wings on high
To a God who cares far more for me
Than for grassy fields and the fair lily?

How much more can He do for me?
When well He's done much already
Faithfully constant with love divine
Grateful am I that He's truly mine

In faith I choose to fret no more
Reminded that lilies have no store;
In His care, life can surely be
Of unmatched grace and liberty

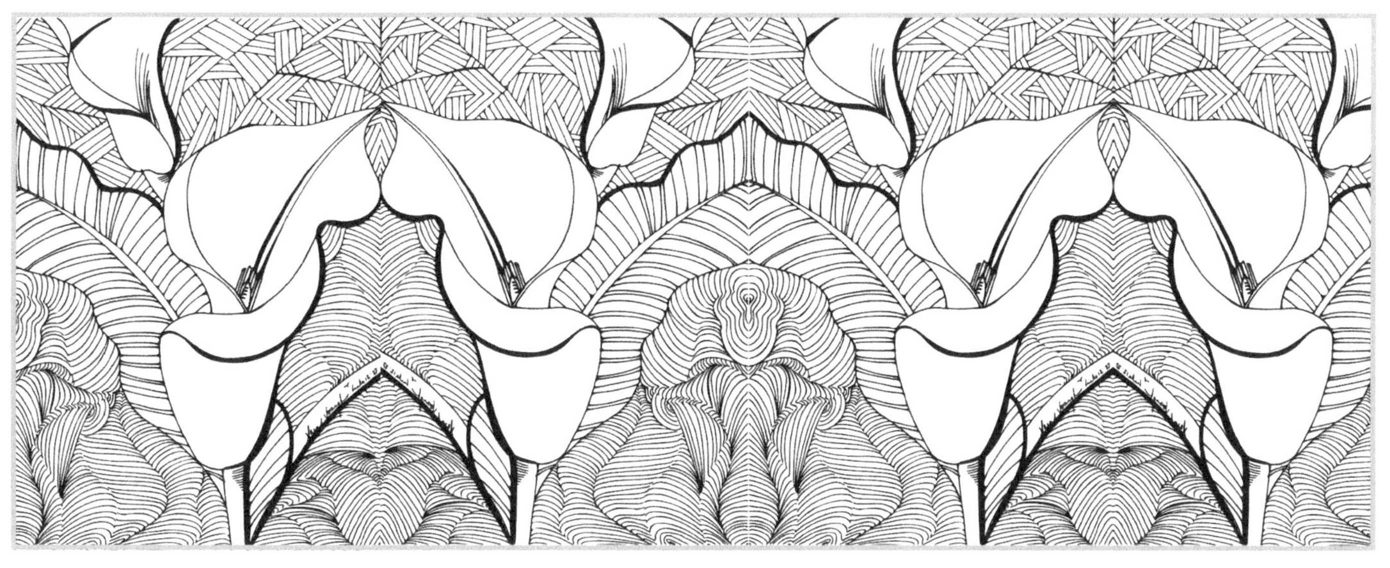

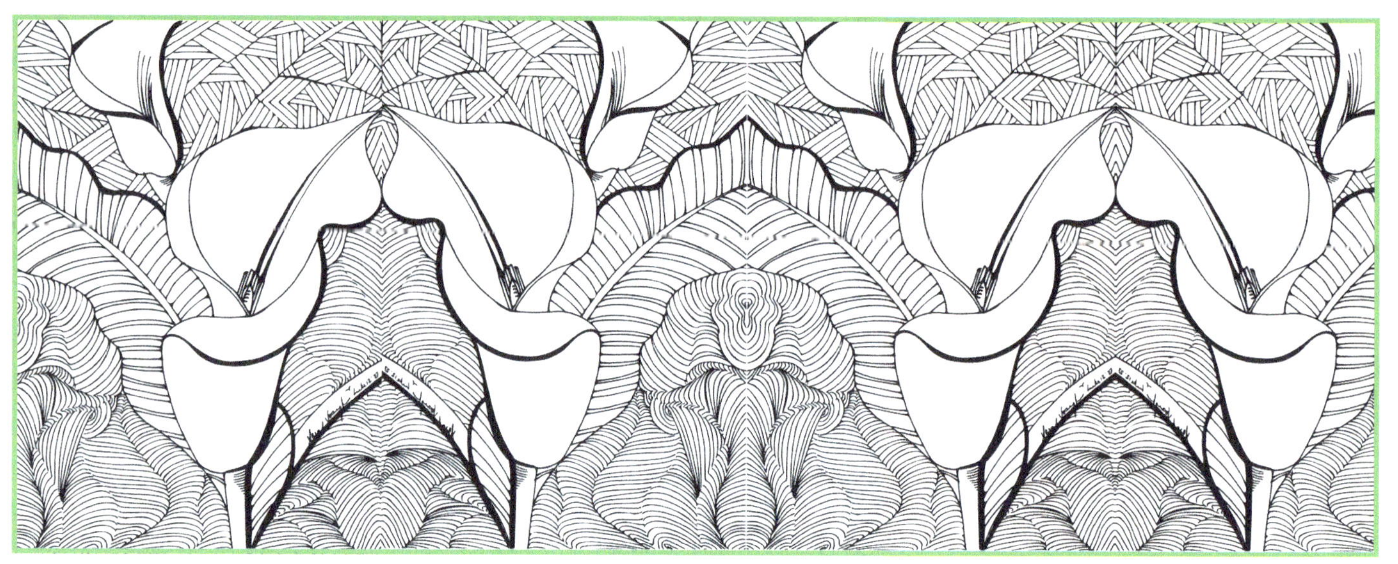

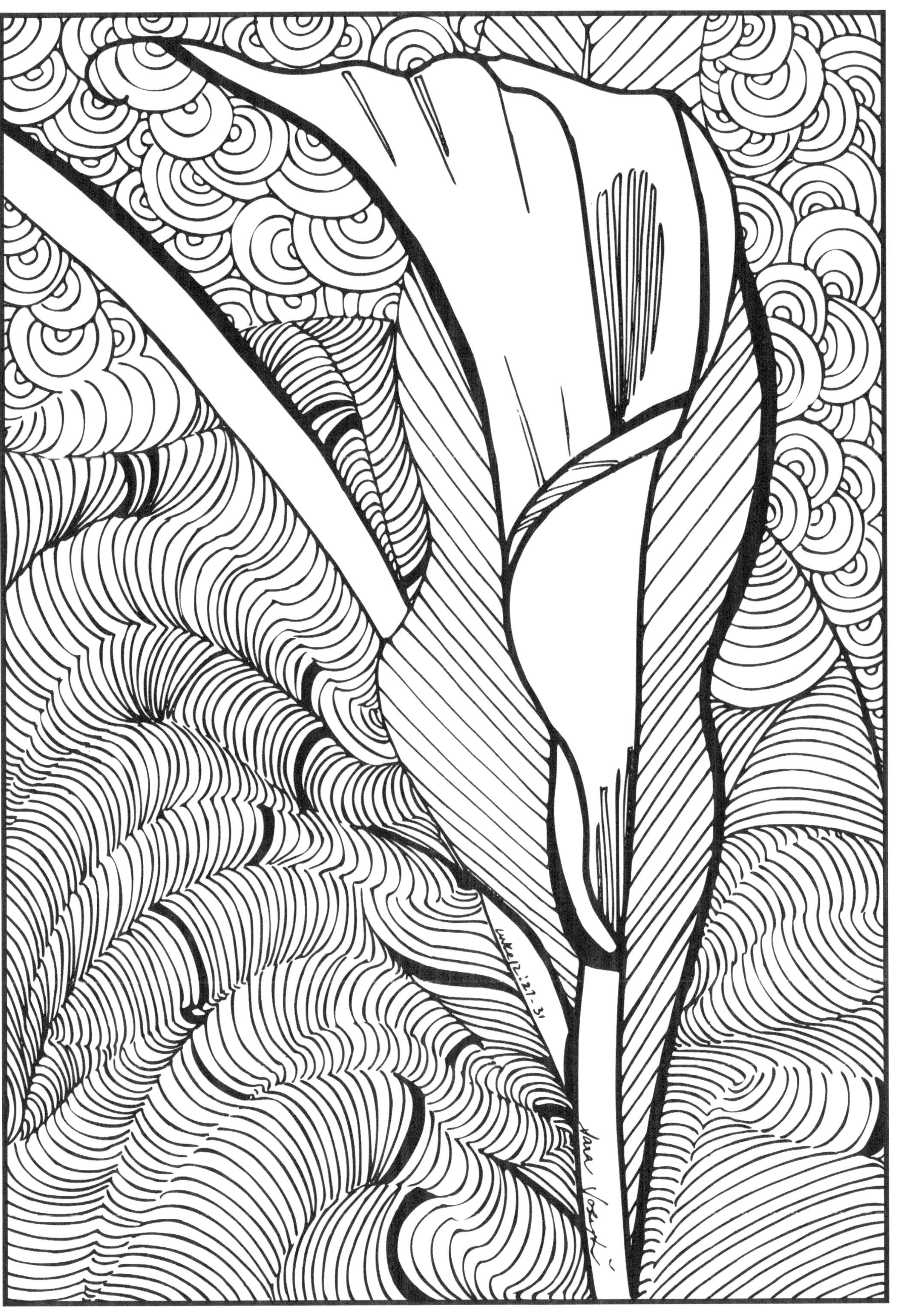

Luke 2:27-31

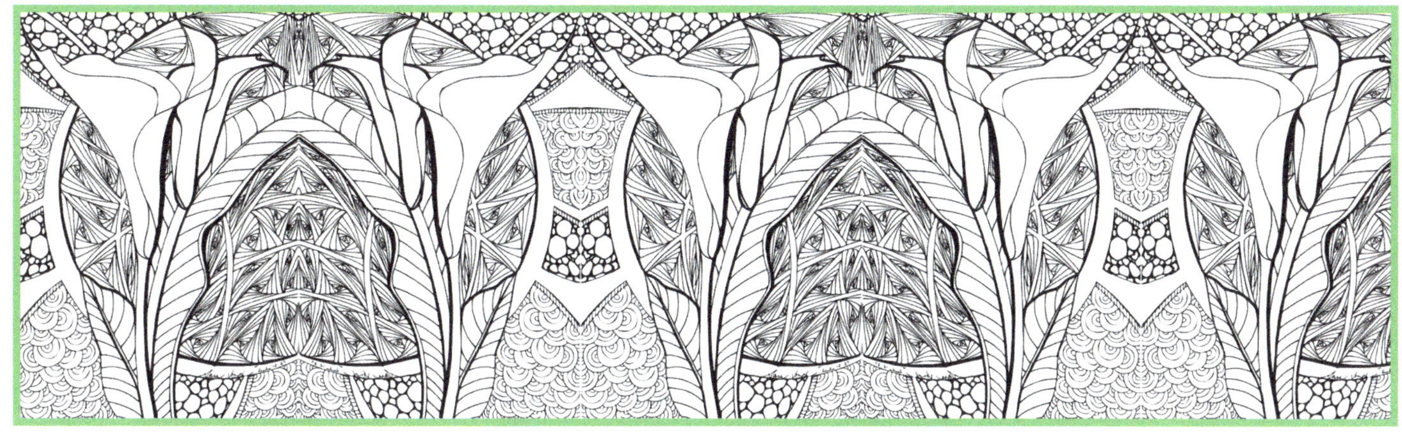

ABOVE ALL WE CAN ASK OR THINK

Jesus asked a question that was deliberately expansive and without limits. "How much more?" Don't allow weak faith to impose boundaries that He never intended.

When we yield in faith to the possibility that God will extravagantly care for us—far beyond what we can conceive then anxiety must become a thing of the past.

"Now unto him that is able to do exceeding abundantly above all that we ask or think,
according to the power that worketh in us,
Unto him be glory in the church by Christ Jesus throughout all ages, world without end. Amen." Ephesians 3:20-21

Journal what more you would like to ask God for. Go ahead, allow your imagination to soar unrestrained.

Notice that "exceeding" was inadequate to describe His ability and desire—"abundantly" was added, and the promise was still found wanting. Neither did "exceeding abundantly above" capture His largesse. Only when the promise included "all we ask or think" did it convey His all-encompassing generosity. Therefore, make big requests! This is the God of the Universe whom you petition. He is your Father, eager to meet your every need with resources beyond your wildest imagining. Trust Him with your future.

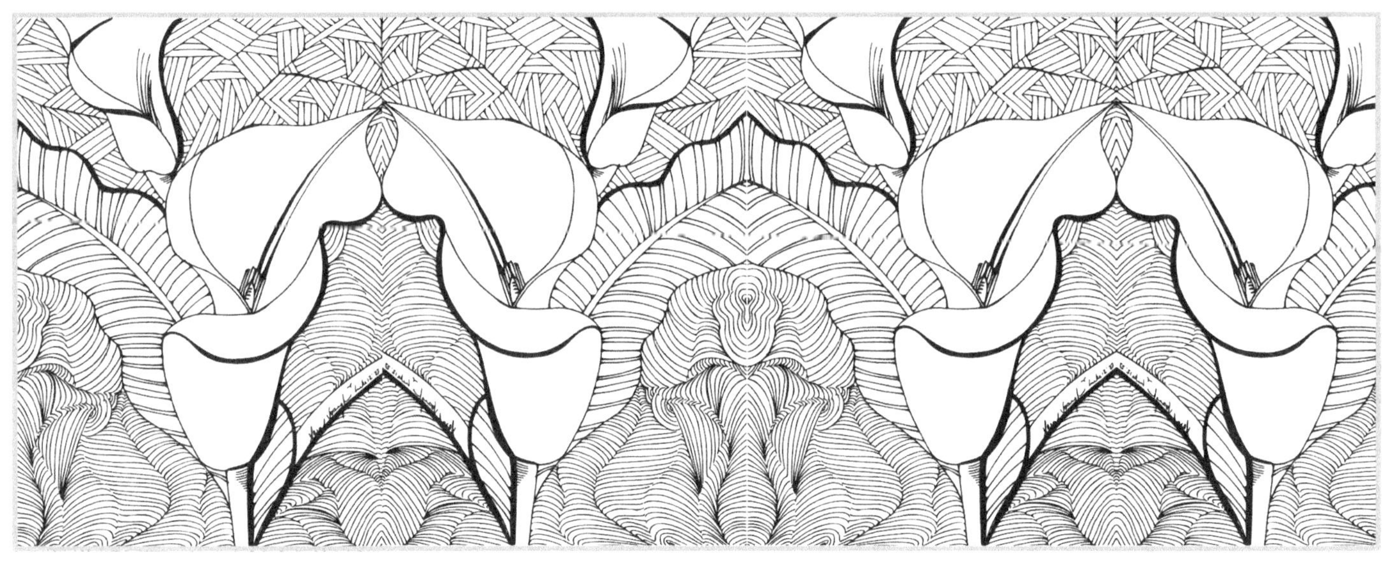

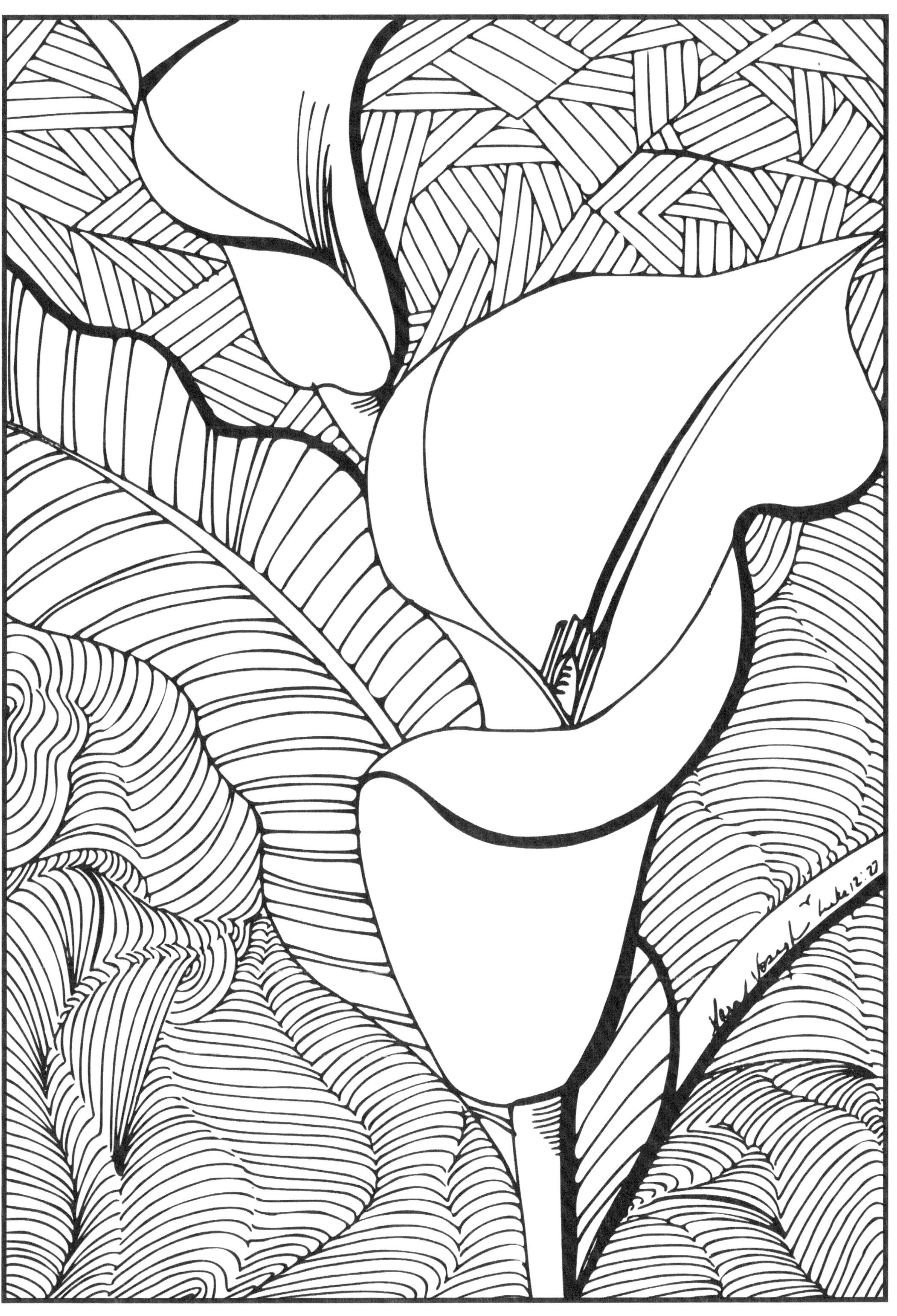

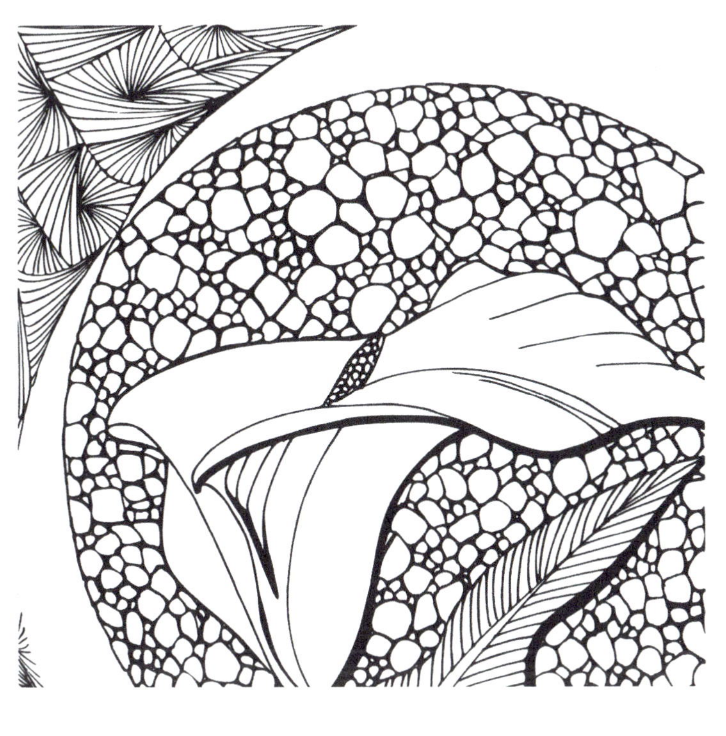

*"And all things,
whatsoever ye shall ask
in prayer, believing,
ye shall receive."
Matthew 21:22*

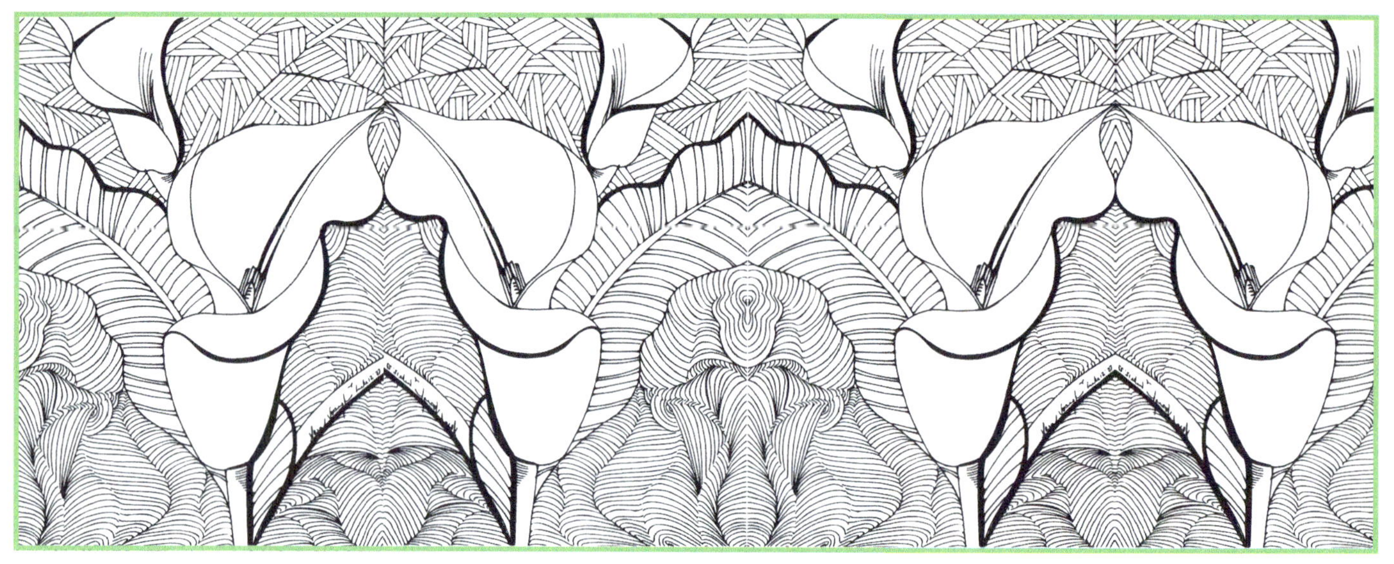

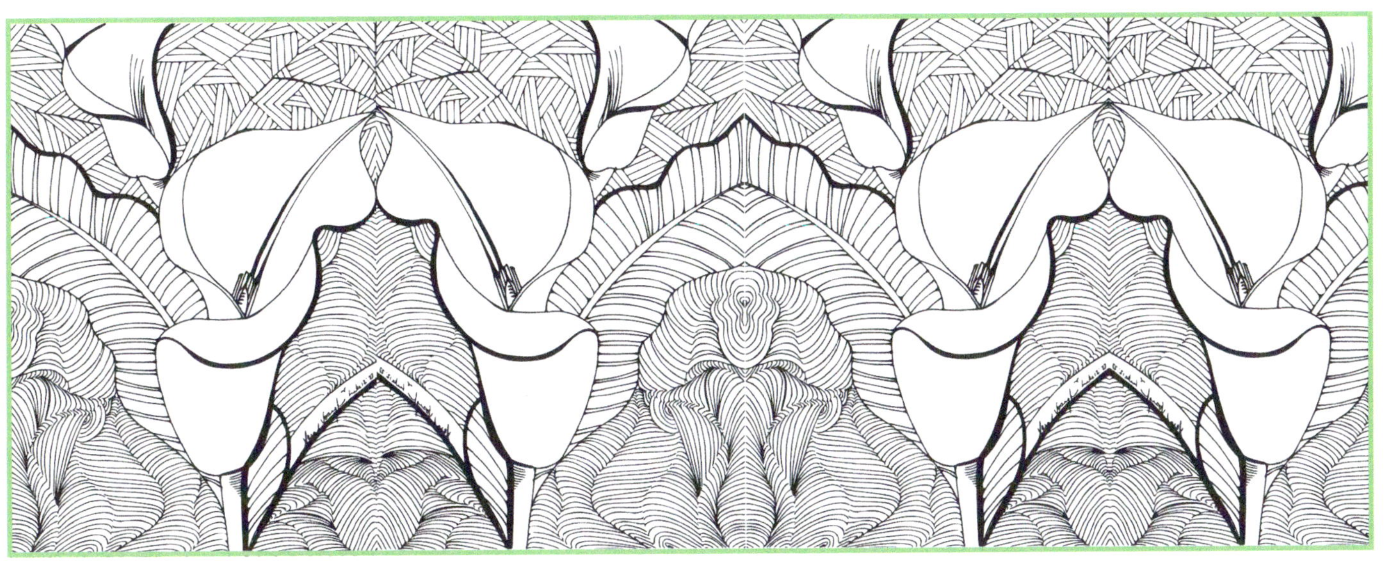

Seek Not

"And seek not ye what ye shall eat, or what ye shall drink." Luke 12:29

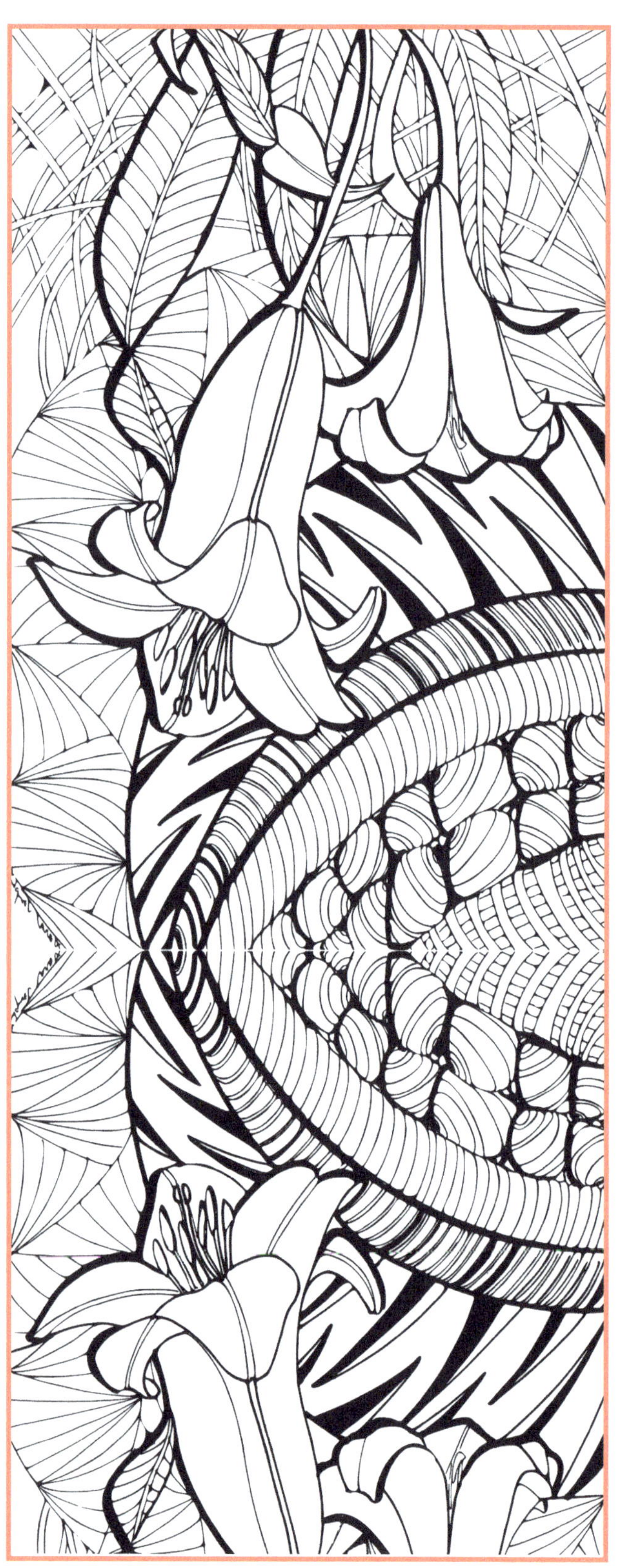

The Rooted Lily

Secure in a patch of chocolate loam

Unable to wander far or roam

Upturned face kissed by the dew

Robed in splendor under the blue

The lily cares not what to eat

Divinely served the finest meat

Would that I be as content

Not toil until I'm wholly spent

Father will care for all my needs

With heavenly manna will surely feed

Happy is a life empty of care

Worry-free and clothed with flair

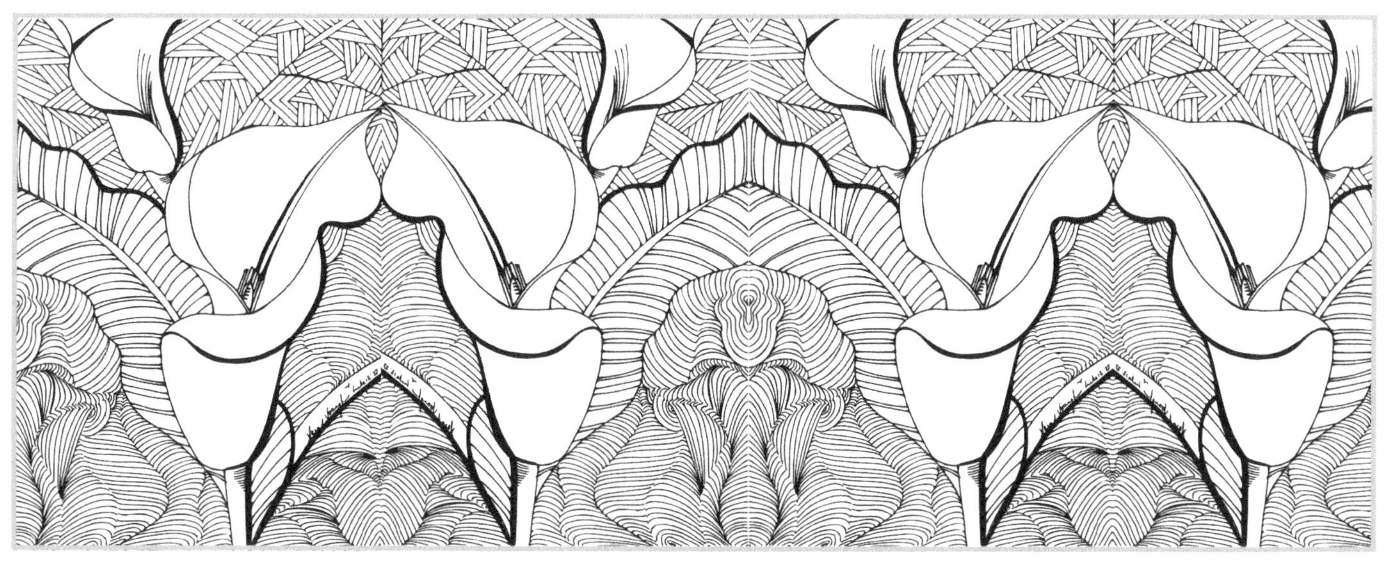

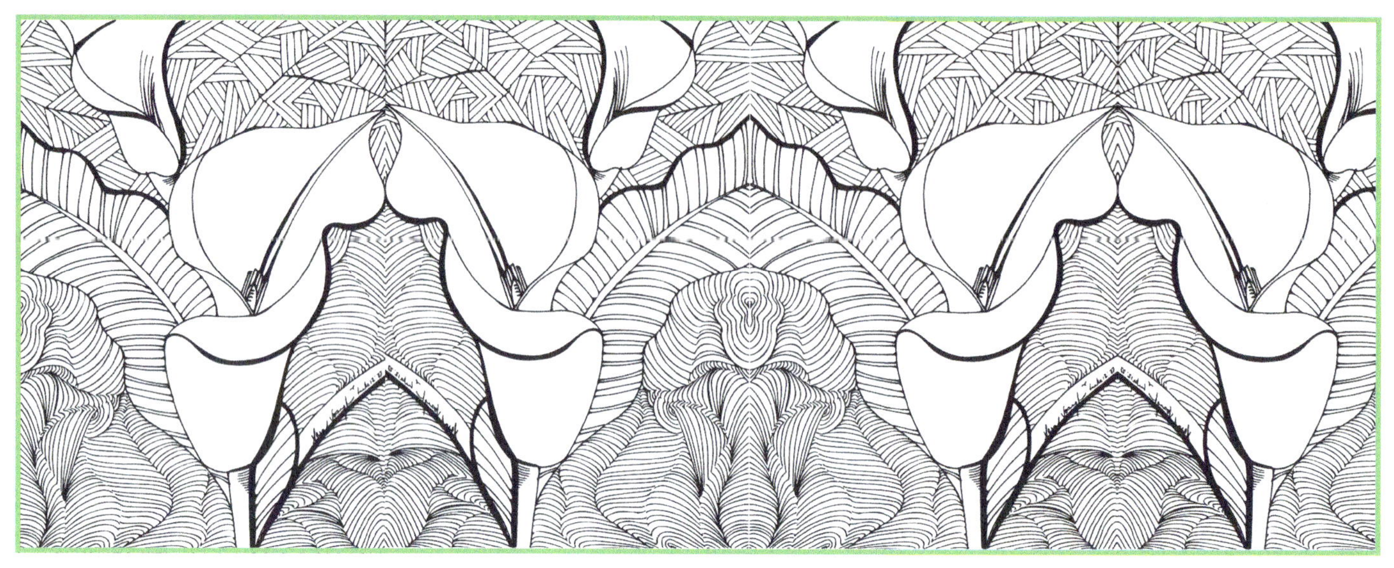

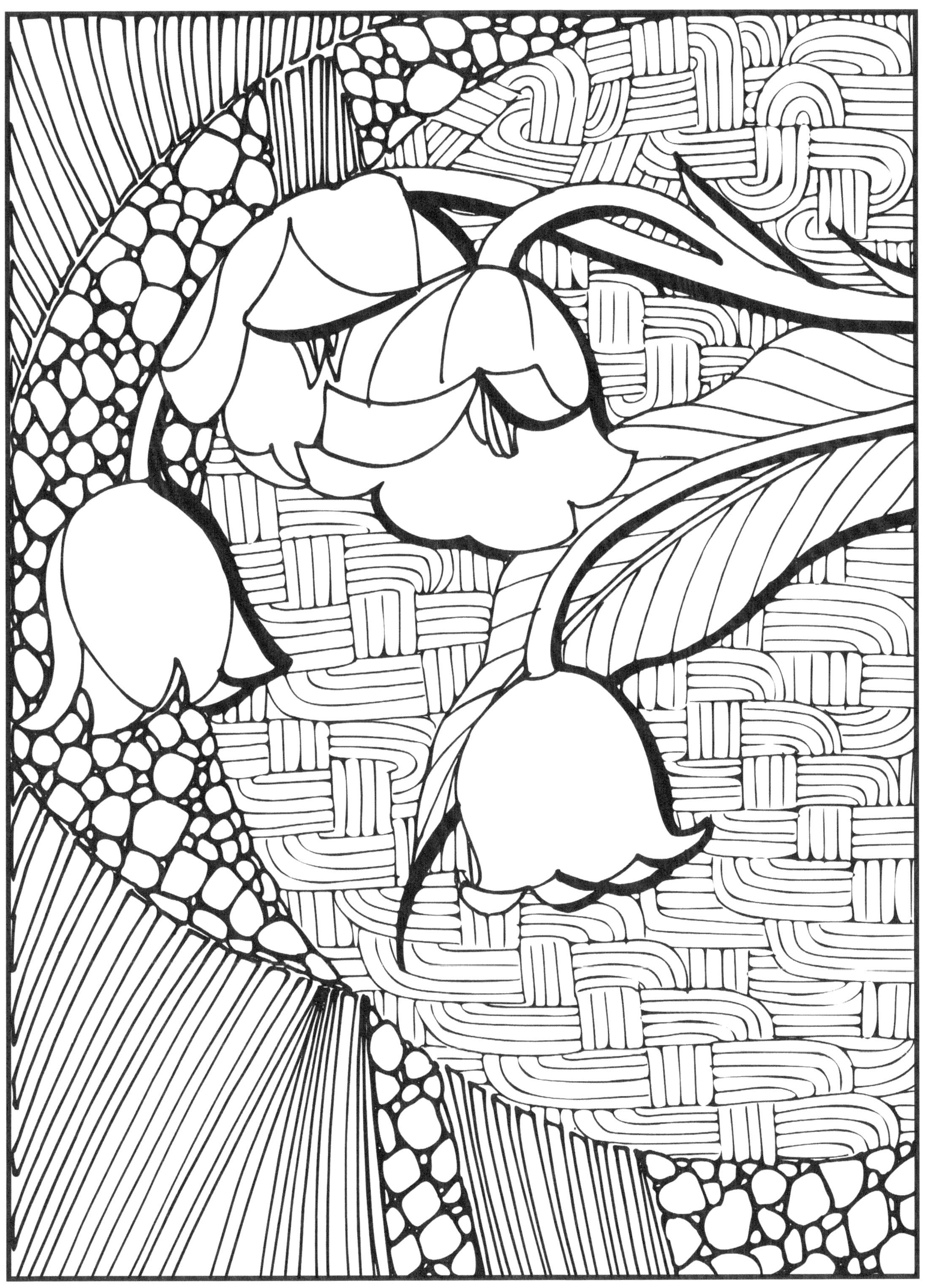

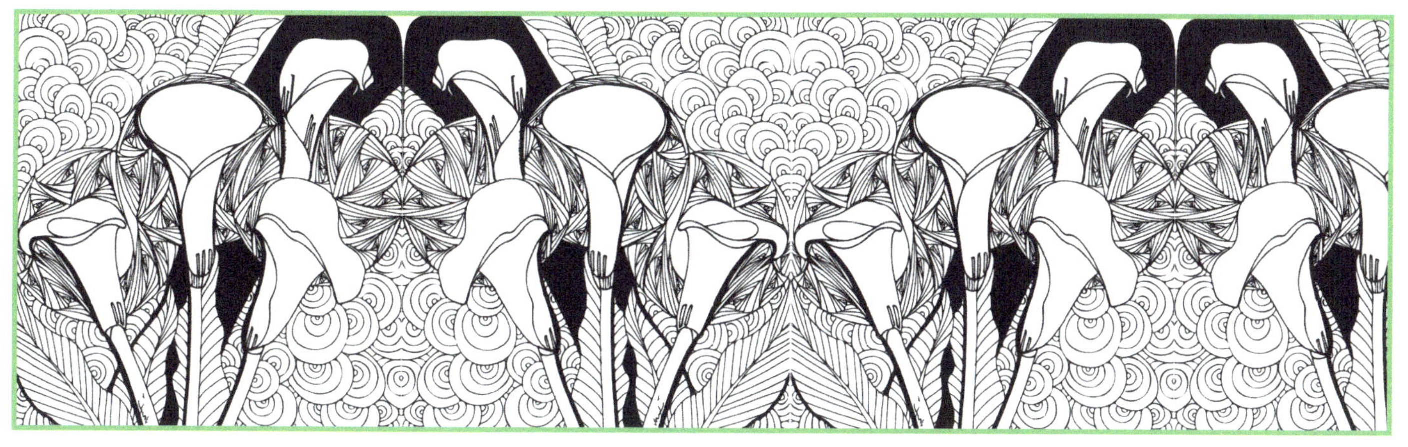

Be Not of Doubtful Mind

Anxious thoughts clamor for attention
Smothering joy and stifling fun
How do I laugh when panic screams
When peace and hope seem only a dream?

"Consider the lily," says the Voice from within
A memory from pages highlighted and thin,
Untroubled is the lily that basks in the sun
Its stunning, stark beauty matched by no one

If alone in a colorless life confined
He urges you, "Be not of doubtful mind."
Honor He pledges, if you honor Him
Trust Him though hope be alarmingly dim

He vows to robe with garments fair
Who steadfastly lean on His certain care
With ease He'll smooth your anxious brow
So don't doubt; the lily shows you how

Cups drinking dew in bright airy meadows
Voluptuous in beauty at each day's close
God's hand in its charm left undisguised
Peace, to Him you're far more highly prized

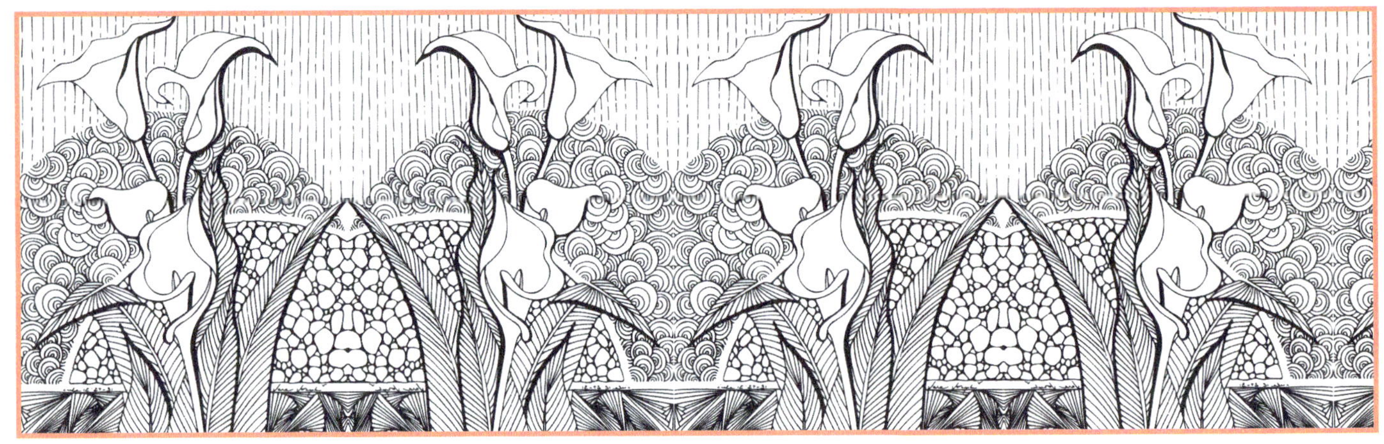

Choose to Be Different

Do you sometimes feel as if life is more than you can handle? Our world is becoming increasingly complex. Everyone is chasing something: a better job, home, car, clothes, vacations ... Innumerable books offer to teach you just about anything you could want to learn, promising wealth, power, fame, and the ever-elusive peace.

It is a game of seek, seek, and seek some more. Few find what they are searching for. Most spend their days in a continuous cycle of seeking without ever finding.

Often those who reach the end of their searches find that the rewards are empty, leaving them yearning for something more. Their victories sour quickly, despite the fact that they are envied for their achievements.

"For all these things do the nations of the world seek after." Luke 12:30

Don't join their ranks. Seek God instead, for a future unlike any other. What He promises has potential that no one has yet fully explored. His ways are infinitely creative.

Decide today to stop seeking for what the nations of the world seek after. Instead I urge you to begin a search for God's way of living, well-supplied, joyous, and content.

Write here what a life like that might look like for you. Be specific and detailed. Make your words a prayer, asking God to fill the gaps that keep you from living such a satisfying life.

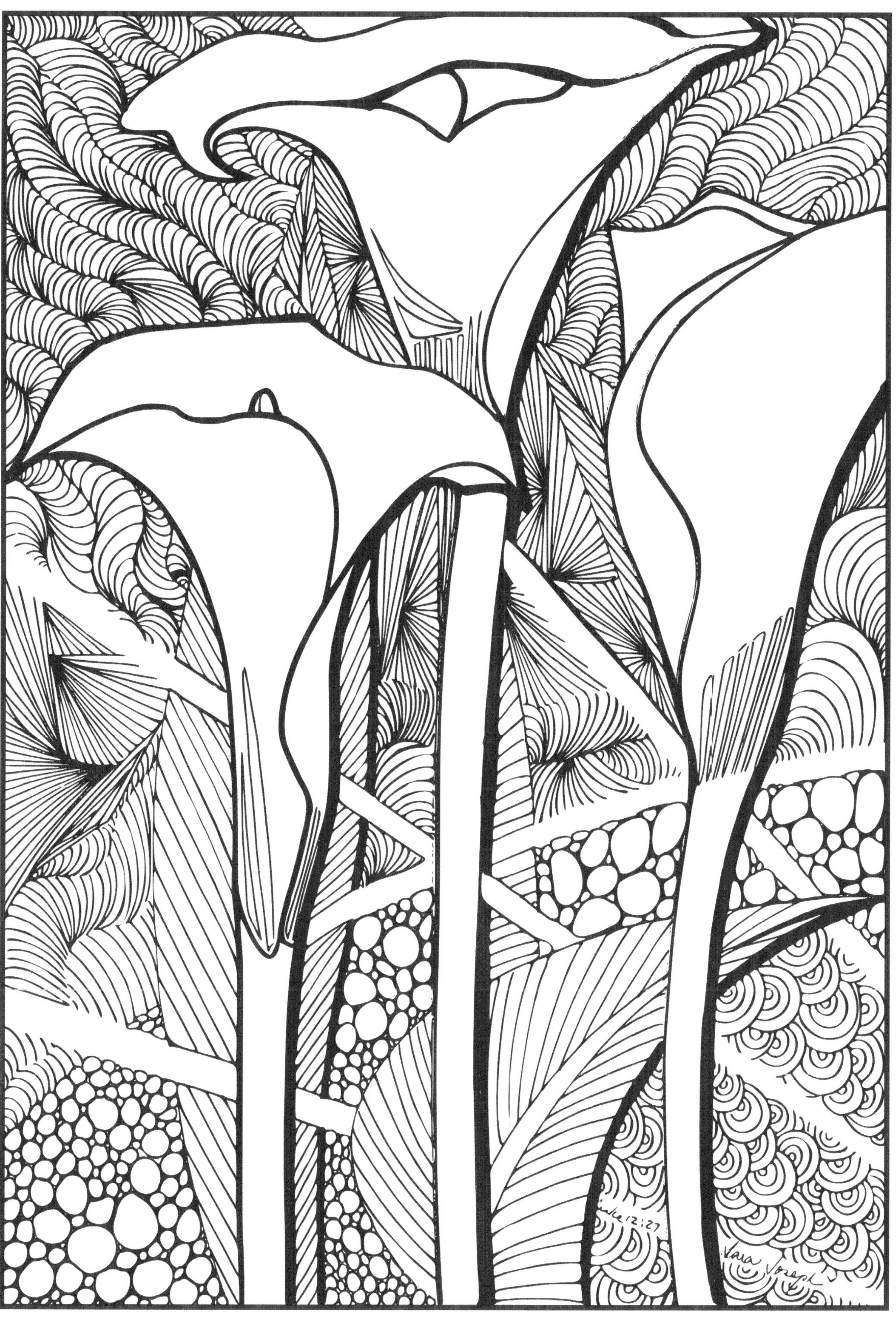

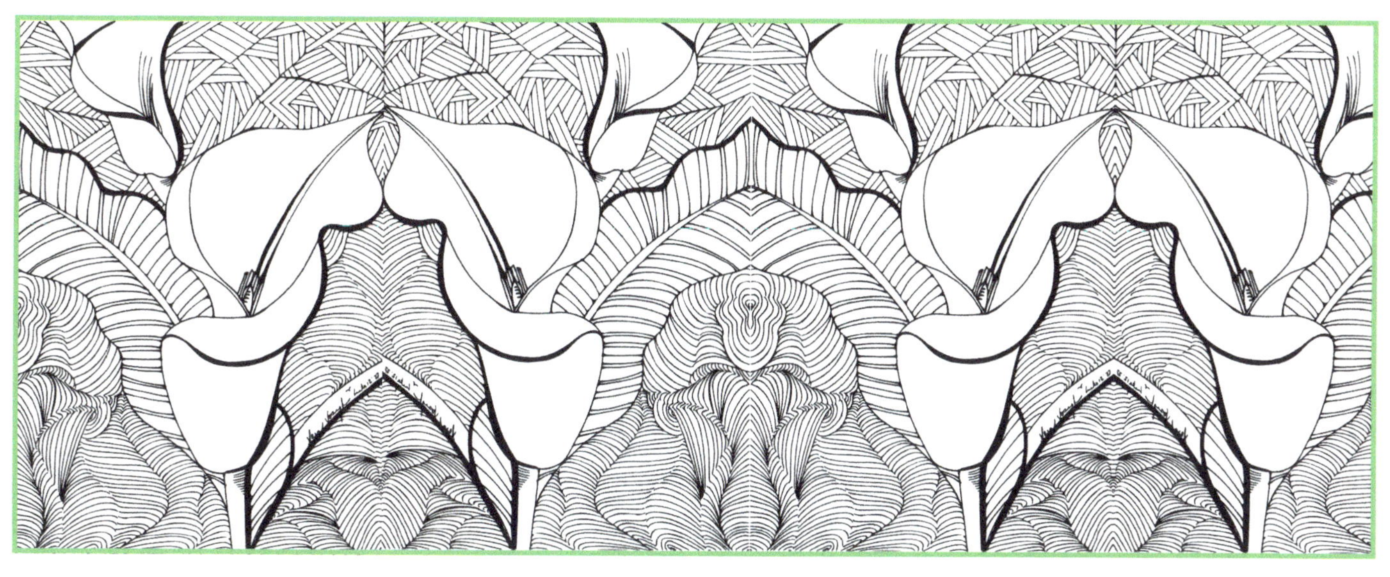

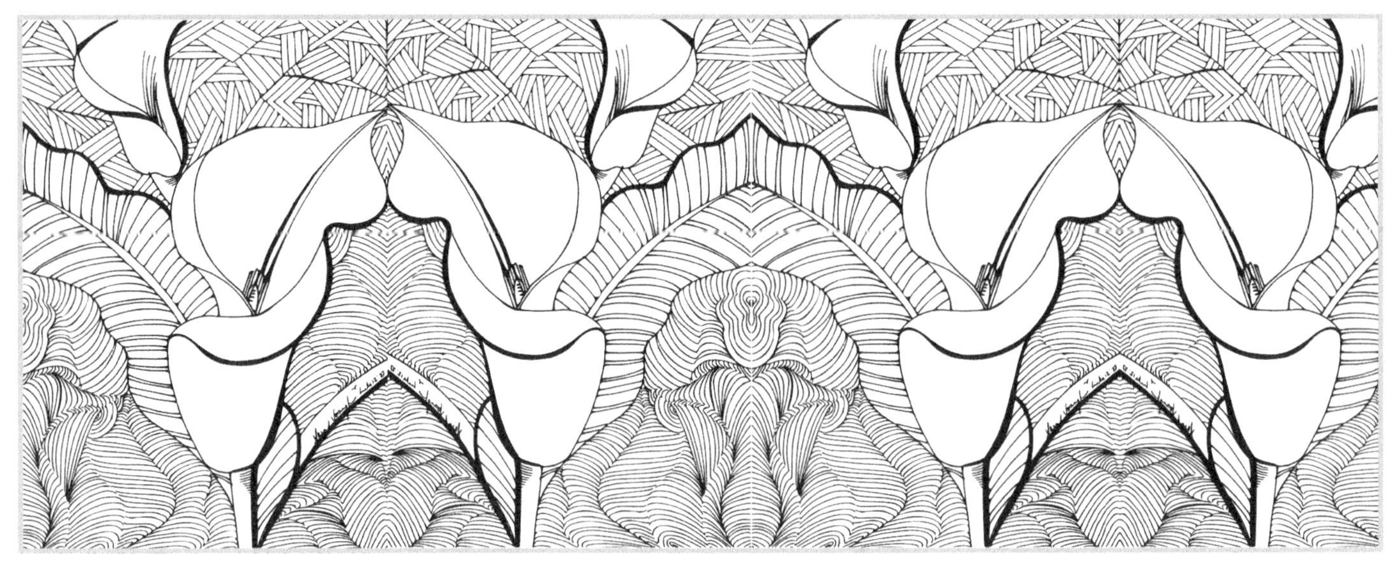

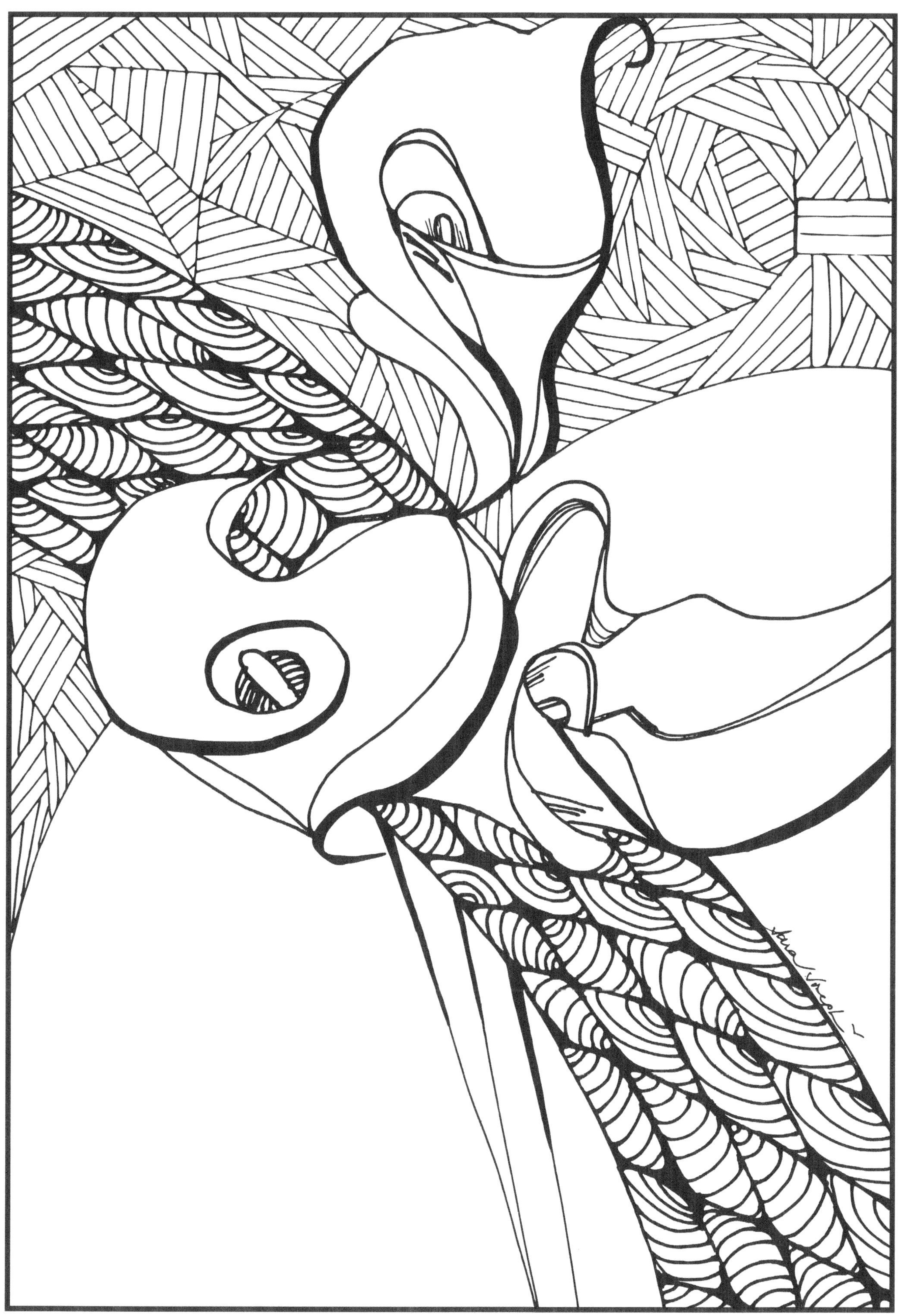

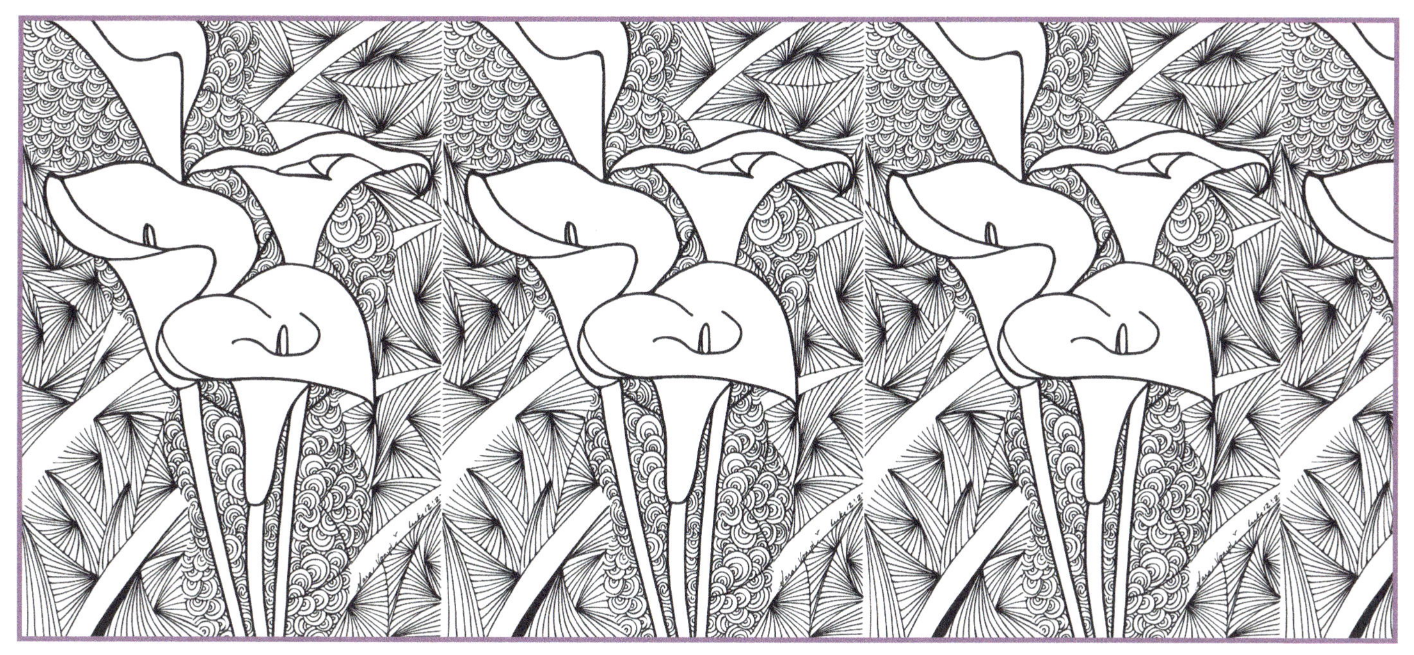

Father Knows Your Need

A dress of hot pink or brilliant blue
Strappy light flats or a well-heeled shoe
"I've nothing to wear!" you loudly groan
Tossing aside clothes sweet with cologne

Lemon chicken or crisply fried fish
Sauced or roasted, just what will it be?
Creamy white pasta or a bland vegan dish
Choices, choices, you're faced with so many

Choose wisely, then, despite the noise
To listen for God and only His voice
And seek His kingdom in all obedience
He'll add to you with wise benevolence

Cherished and tended by Father alone
A life framed by virtue, while blessings pursue
Where selfish pettiness is firmly dethroned
His kingdom to scck is to scc lifc ancw

"Your Father knoweth that ye have need of these things." Luke 12:30

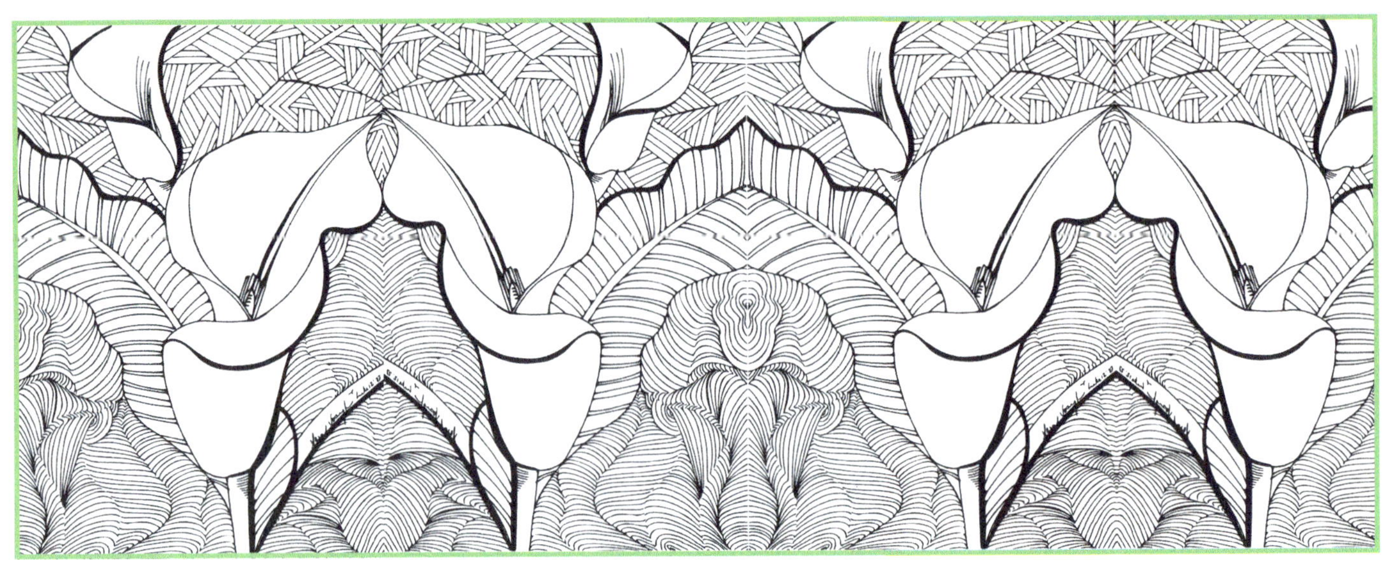

Overwhelmed? Ask Your Father for Help

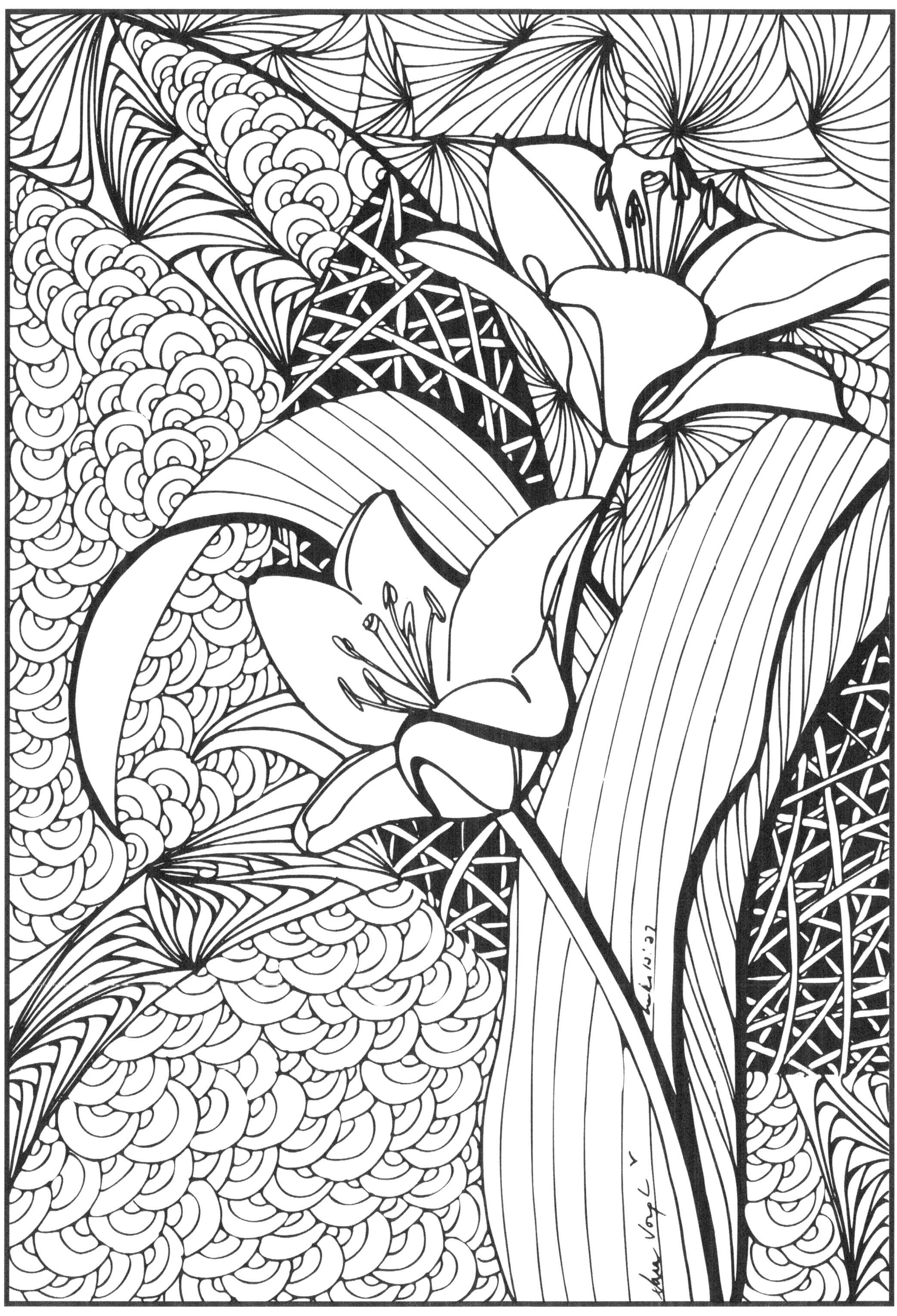

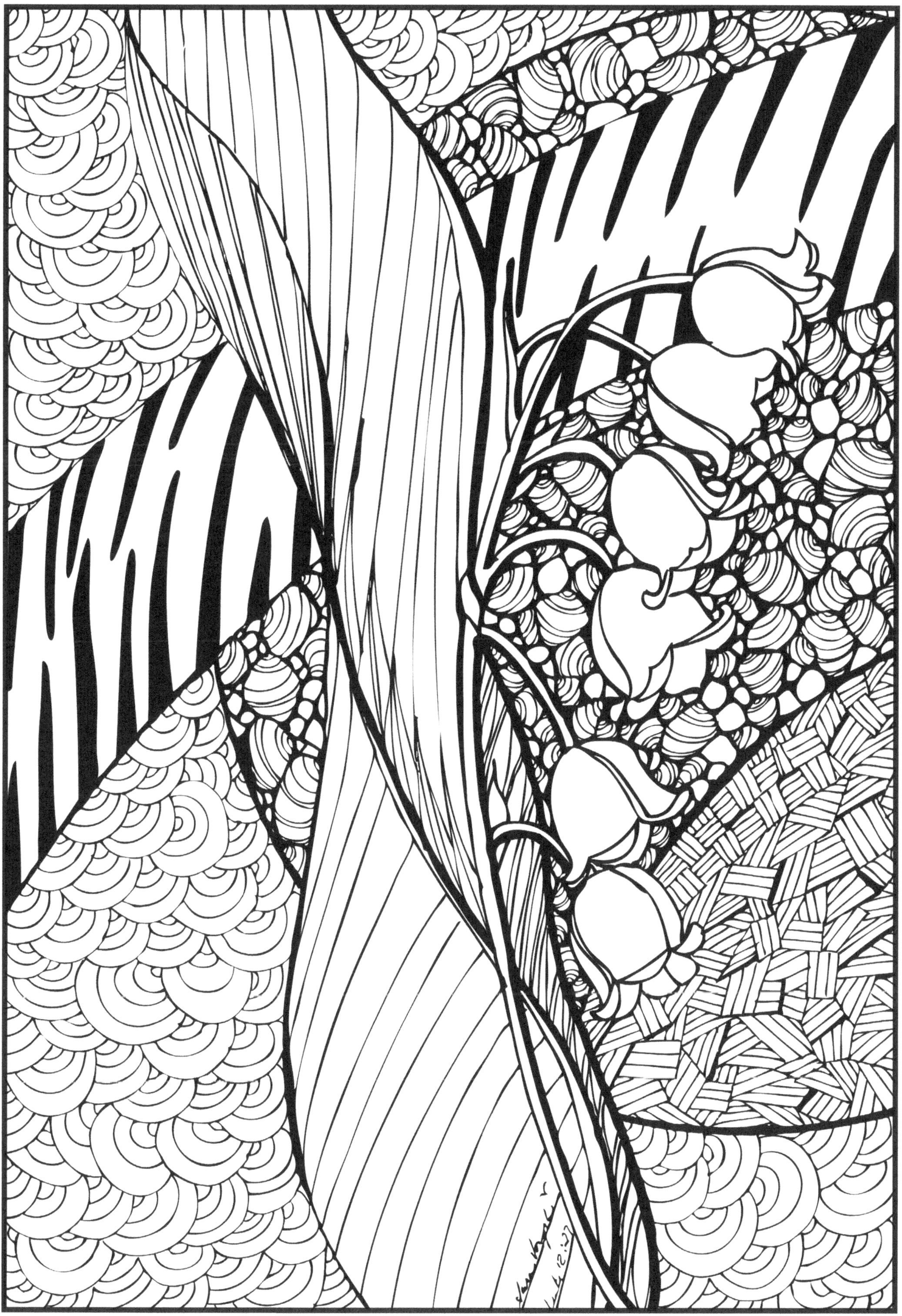

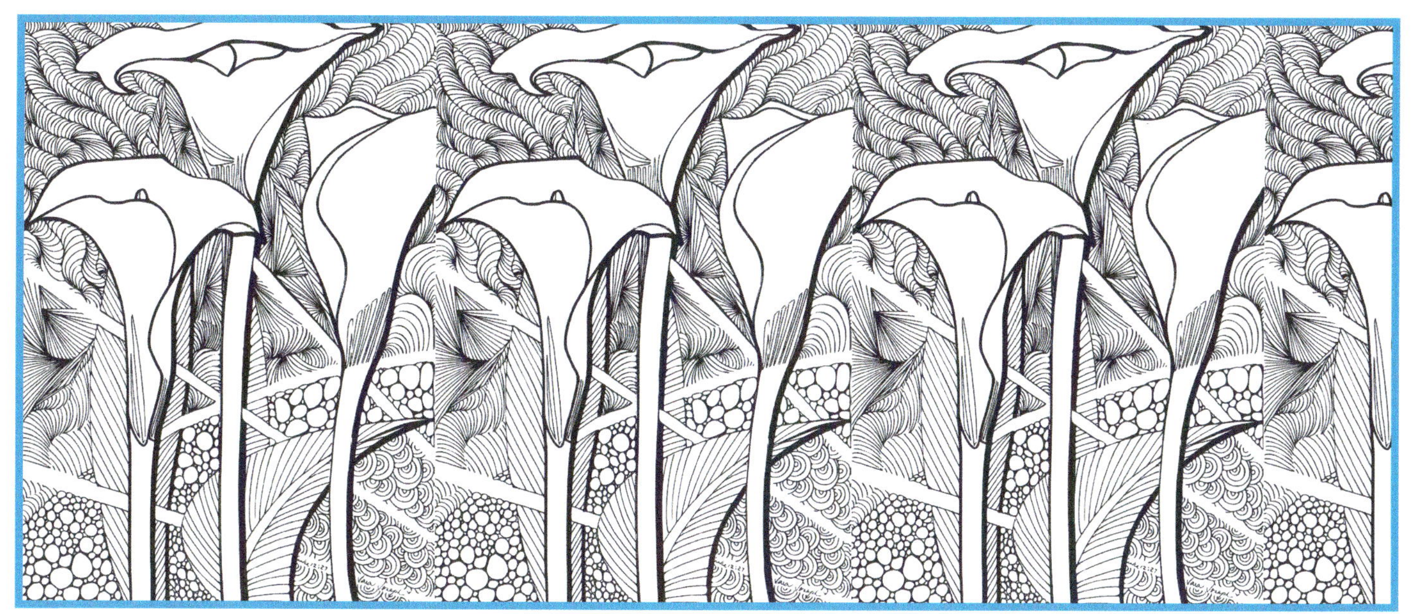

Seek First

Being first in all, I do adore
To be second or third, I do deplore
Hence with each breath I labor to build
A life just for me that I feather and gild

Yet now I learn that I must seek first
This kingdom that seems unrehearsed
Sought with passion and obedience
Of righteousness and much diligence

What I will must be second or third
With first reserved for God and His Word
Then all the stuff for which I once slaved
Will become a memory of what I craved

Added in abundance is all I could need
While in seeking first what He decreed
I haven't now time to seek elsewhere
He has satisfied me with His able care

"But seek ye first the kingdom of God, and his righteousness;
and all these things shall be added unto you." Matthew 6:33

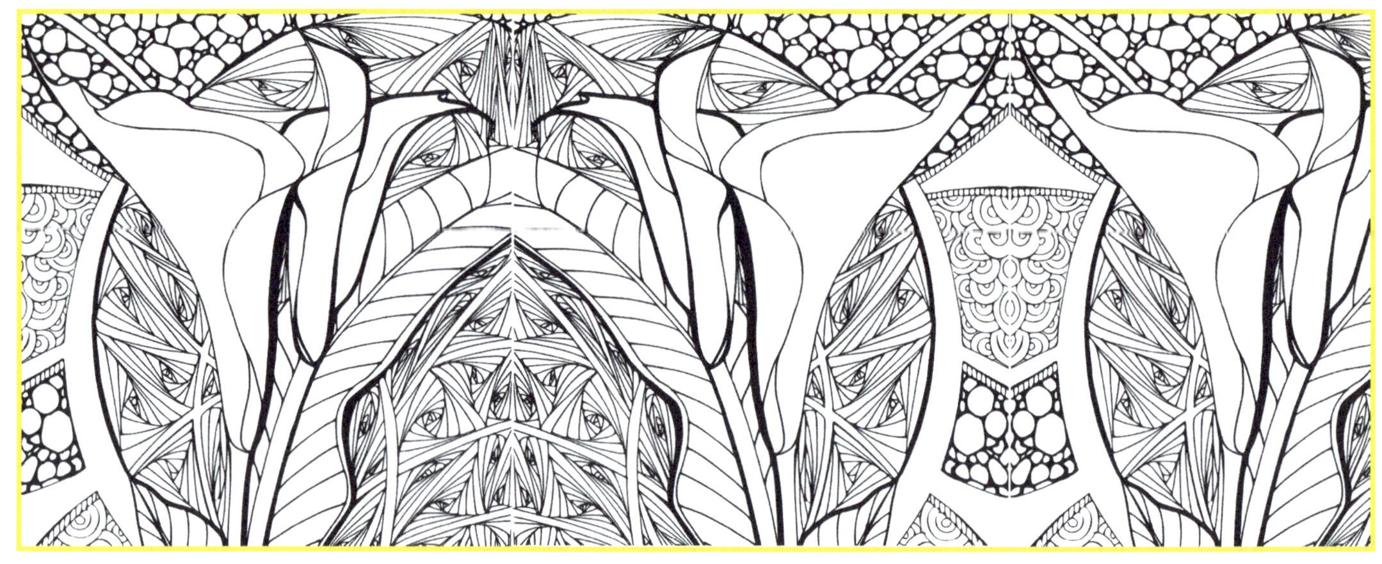

Lay It Down!

Do you nurse grudges against those who have wronged you? Avoid the pollution of hatred, anger, bitterness, and regret. Dwelling on and feeding those emotions will most certainly keep you out of this wonderful kingdom that Jesus has promised. Instead, choose to walk in love, forgiveness, kindness, and hope. Remember that enjoying the benefits of this kingdom is a moment by moment decision. This is an unrehearsed life that you alone can walk out by your unique choices.

In your own words, empty yourself of resentment against anyone who has hurt or harmed you. Come clean; it is worth it! This is a choice that no one can make but you. Do it now to enjoy a future that is uncorrupted by ill will toward another.

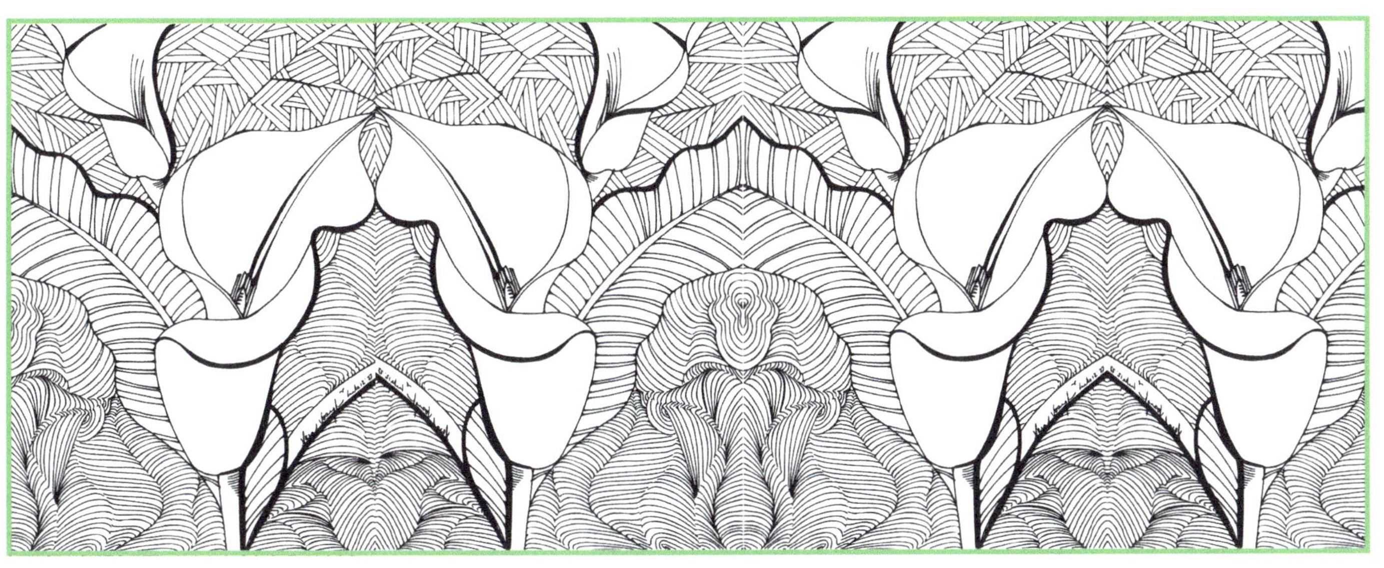

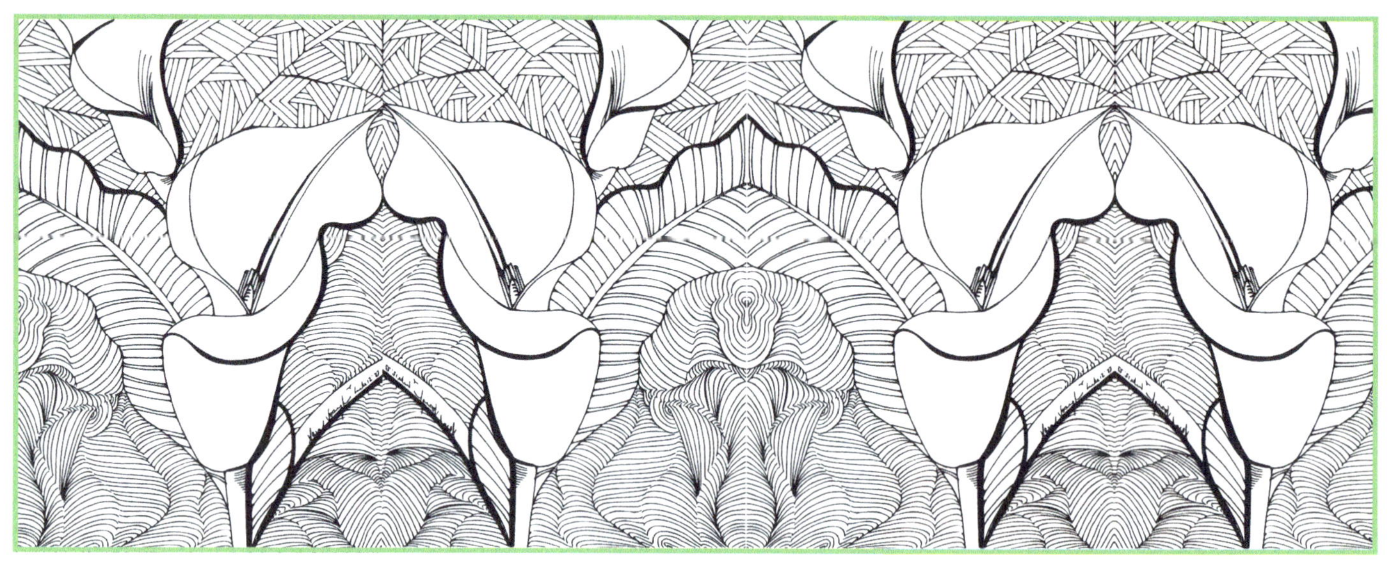

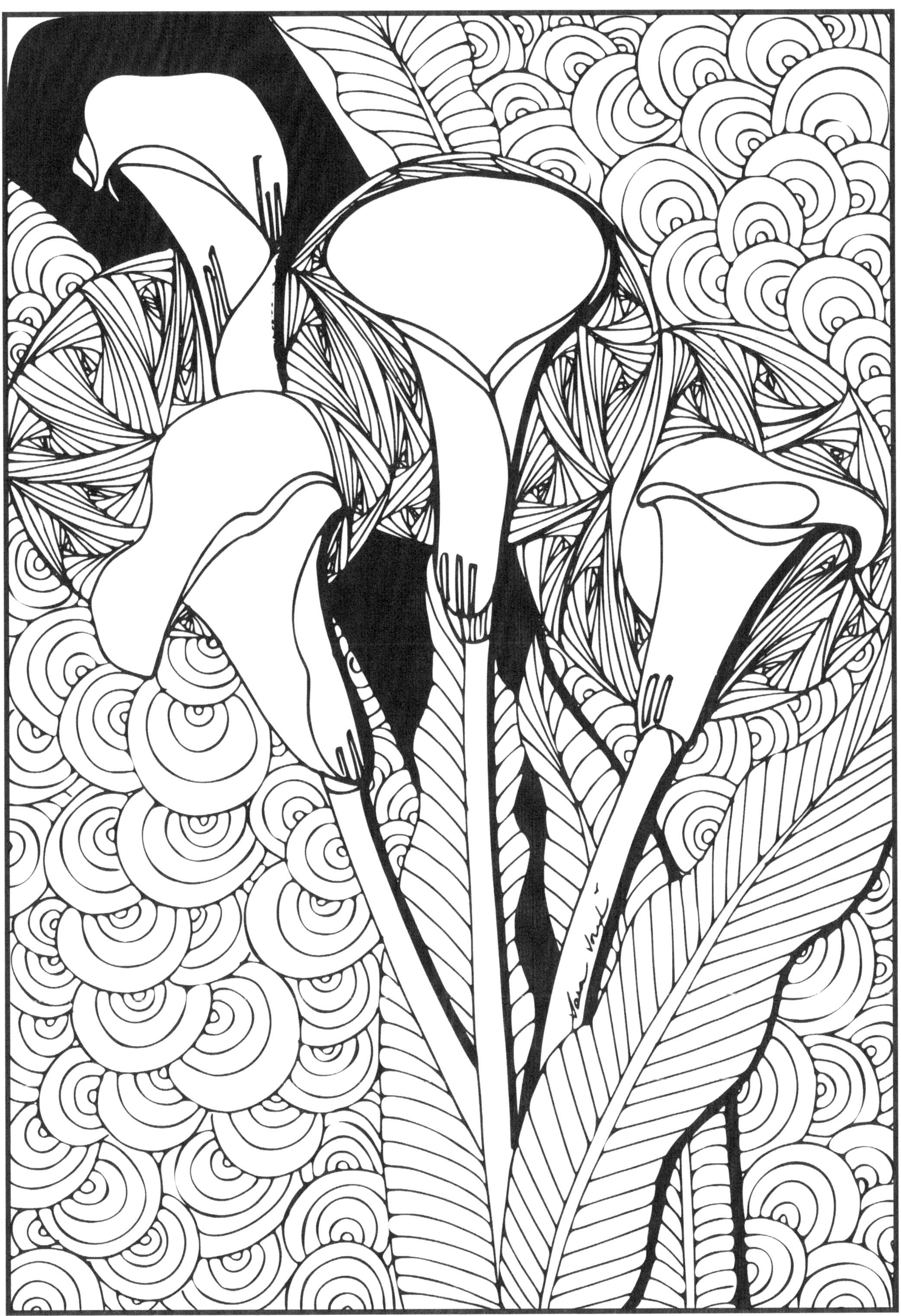

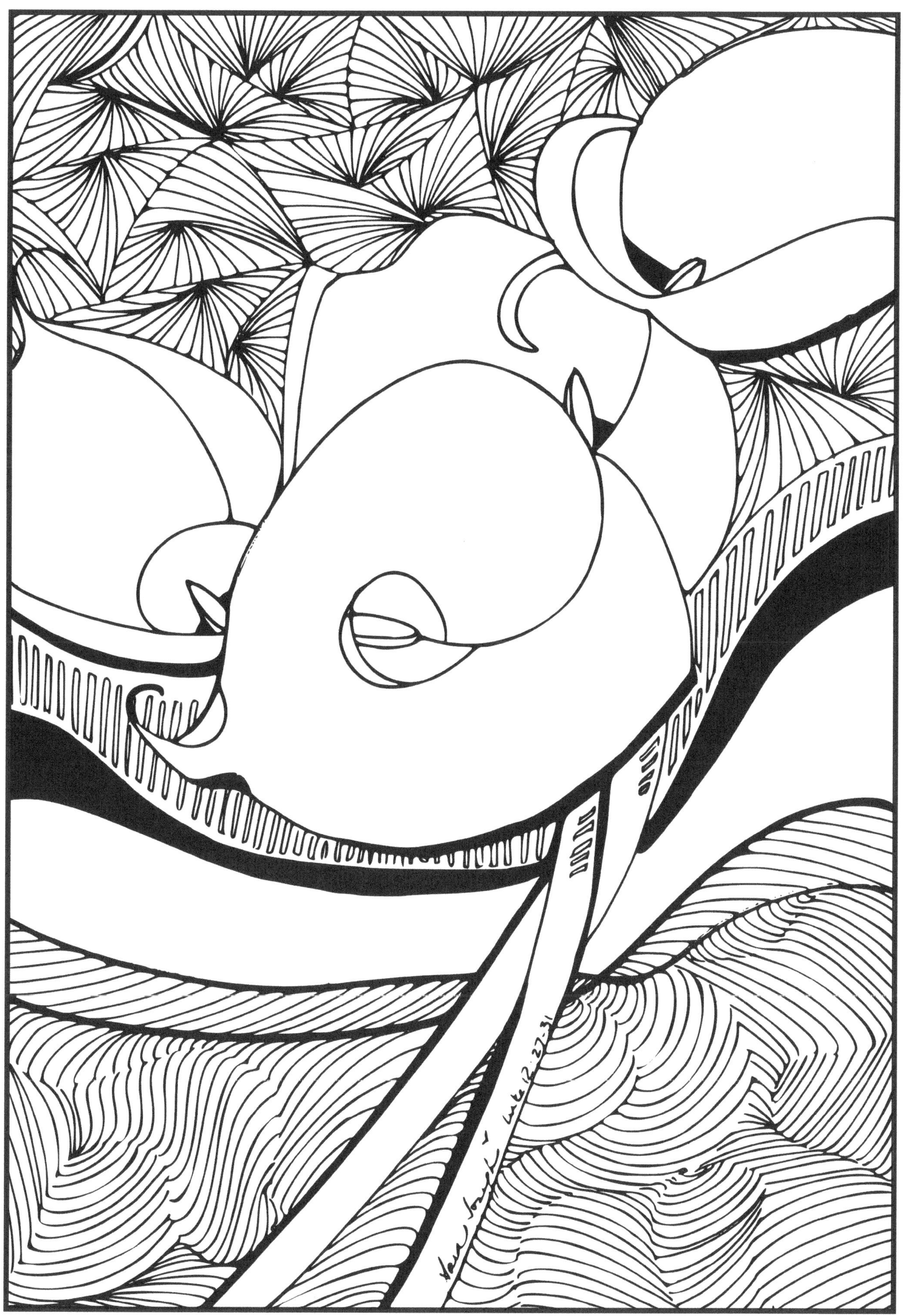

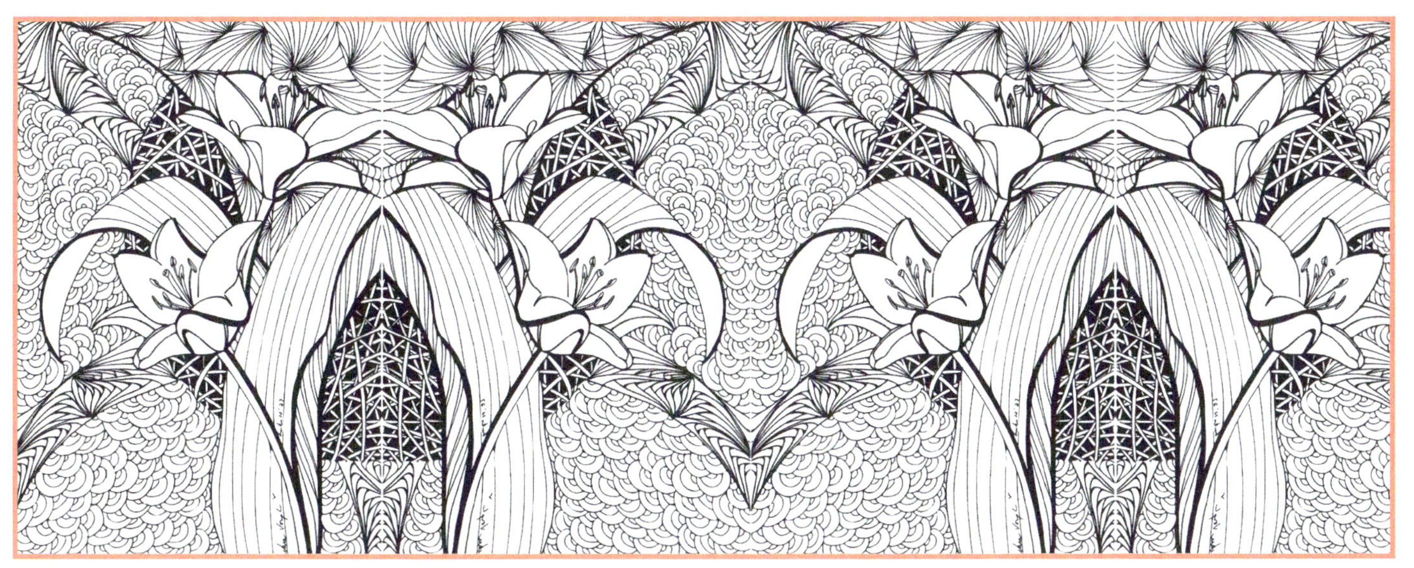

FEAR NOT

God finds great pleasure to give to you

Keys of a kingdom not for a few

With His power and great authority

A jubilant life with no scarcity

Fear has no place within its gates

Your future is not left up to fate

Trust Him, His care is extravagant

Watchful over how your days are spent

Intrepid and free, safely roam far

Dare to chase the farthest star

As one of His own under the sun

No foe can beguile, harm, or stun

"Fear not, little flock; for it is your Father's good pleasure
to give you the kingdom." Luke 12:27-32

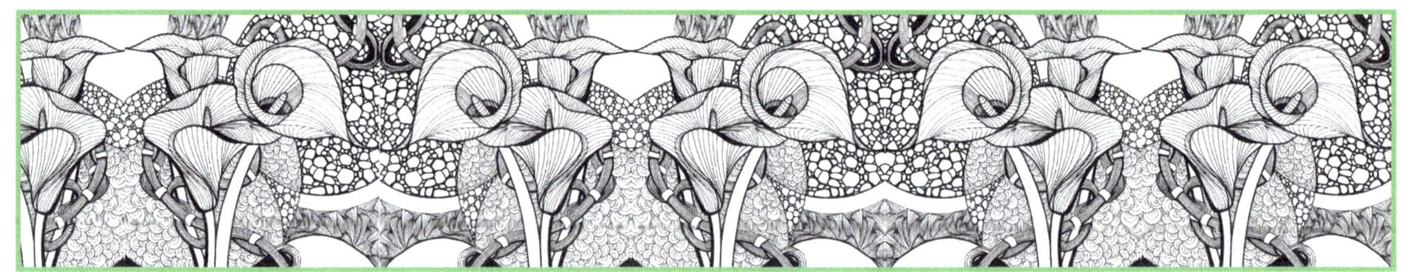

WILL YOU OBEY?

Nothing can suck the life out of you like fear can!

What is your greatest fear today? Don't write it down!

Fear contemplated will become magnified, growing like the monsters of horror movies. Once uncapped and loosed, fear will be impossible to recapture and contain. Don't give a voice to fear, not even in your thoughts.

"Fear not!" is an often repeated command in the Bible. For Christians eager to please God, this is a command to take seriously. Failure to comply will result in a defeated life.

So don't yield to fear. Submit instead to God's Word with its many wonderful promises; then rise up. He has a glorious life ahead for you! Purpose to live it well by faith. Write out your commitment to refuse fear wherever it rears its ugly head.

Do a word search in your Bible for *fear* and list some of your favorite verses that encourage you to live fearlessly, trusting in the Lord.

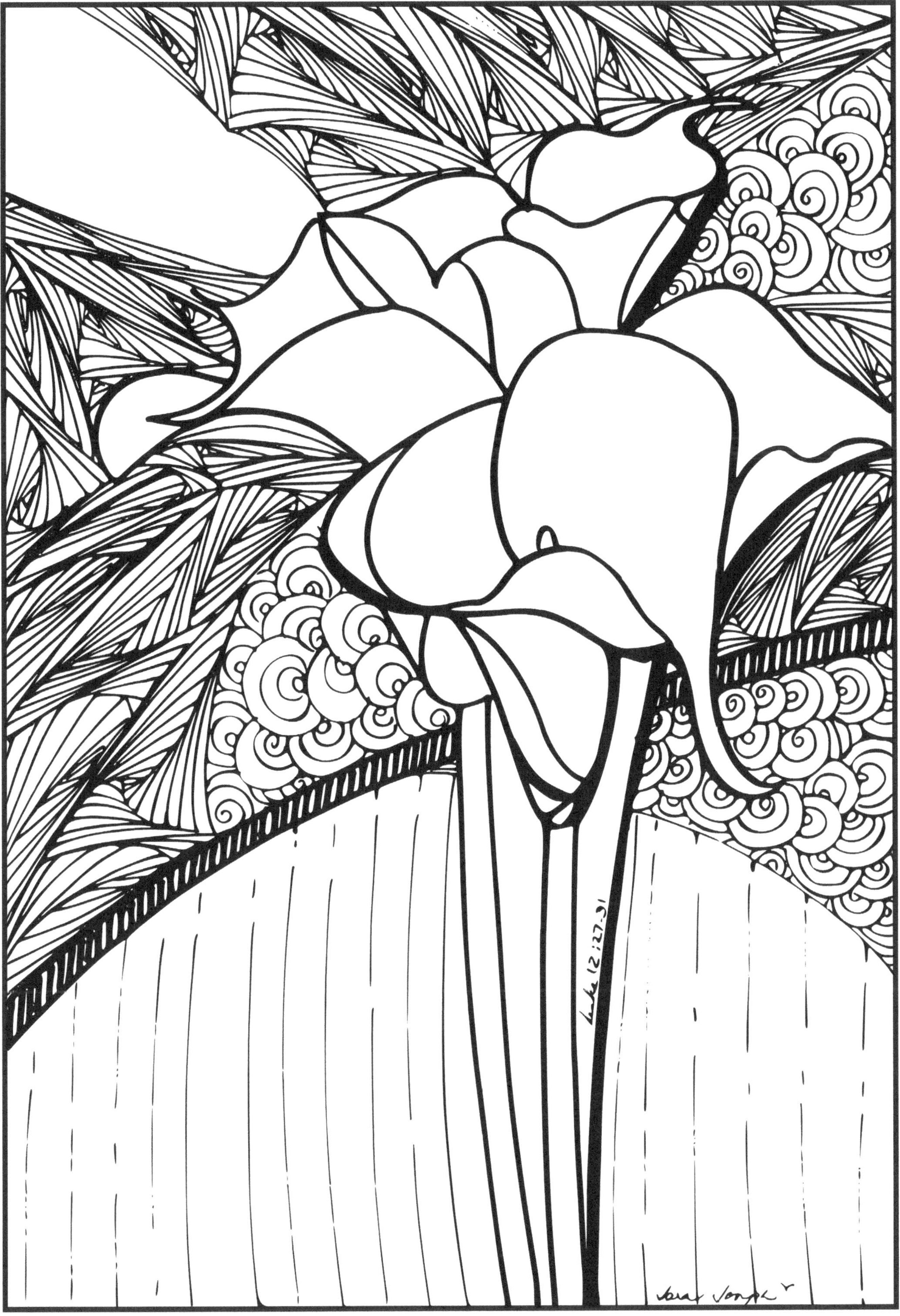

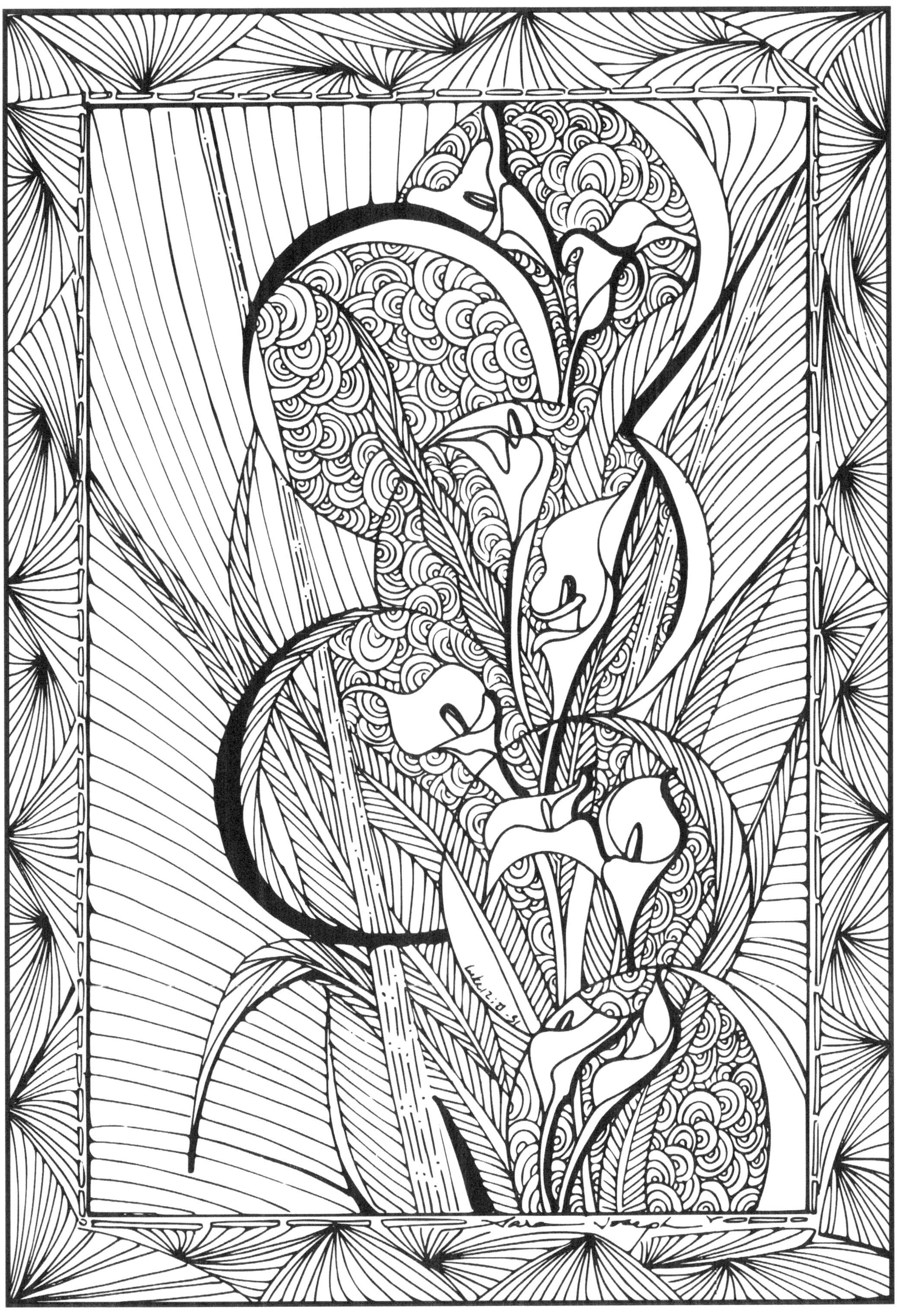

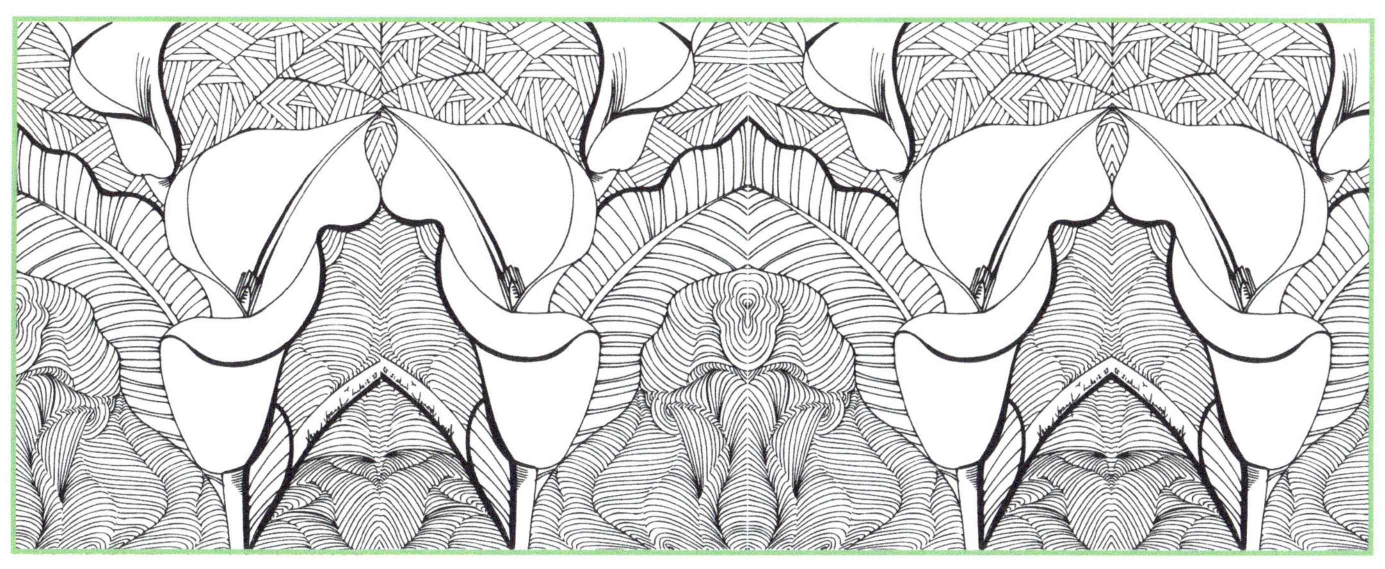

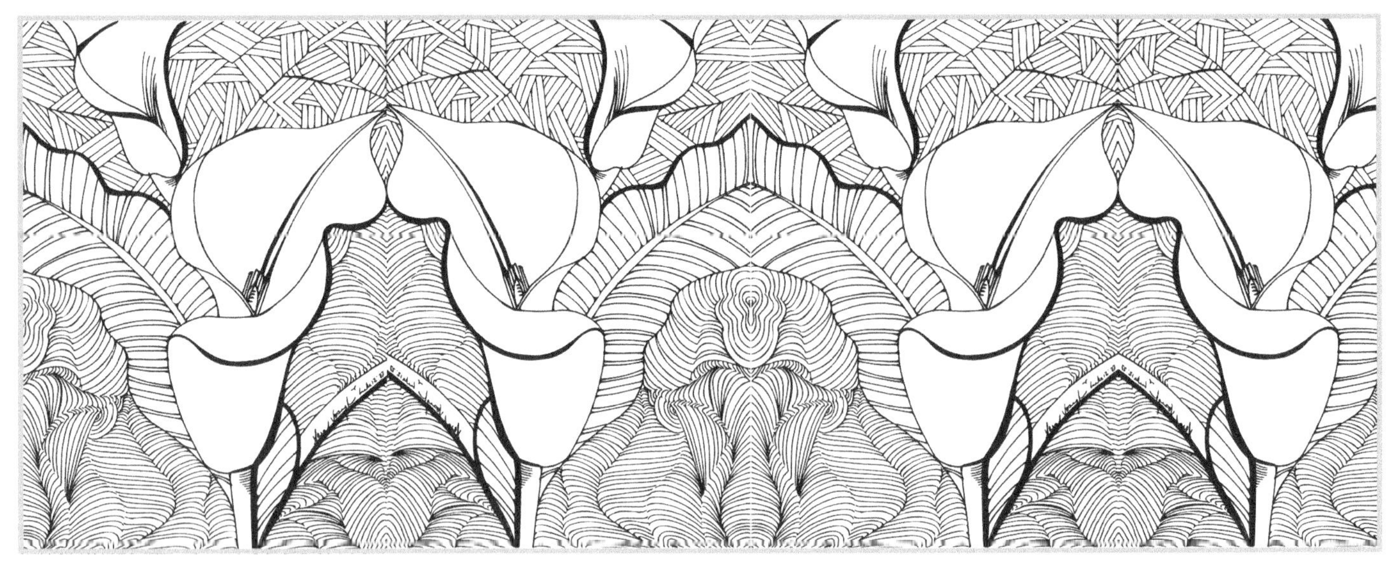

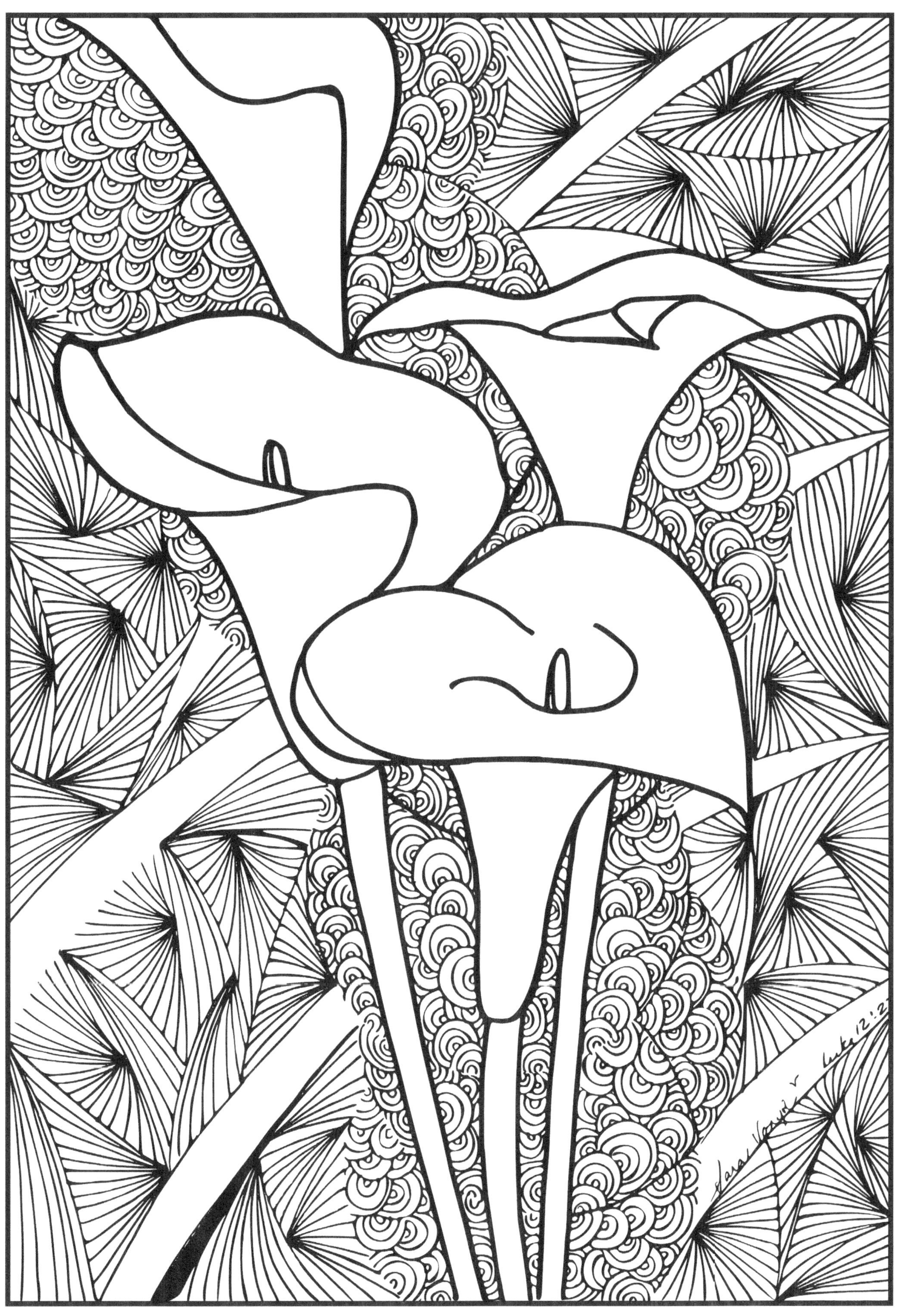

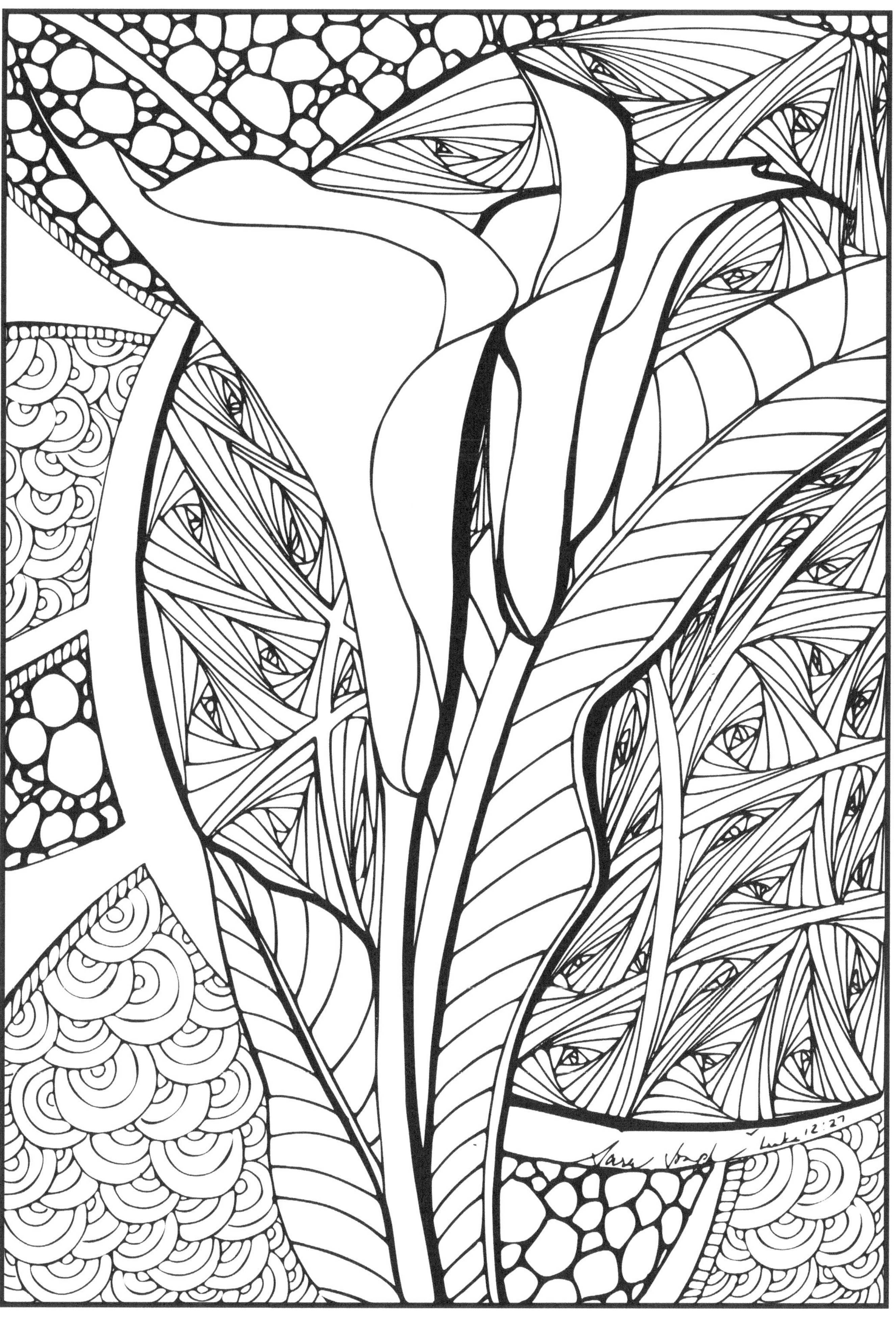

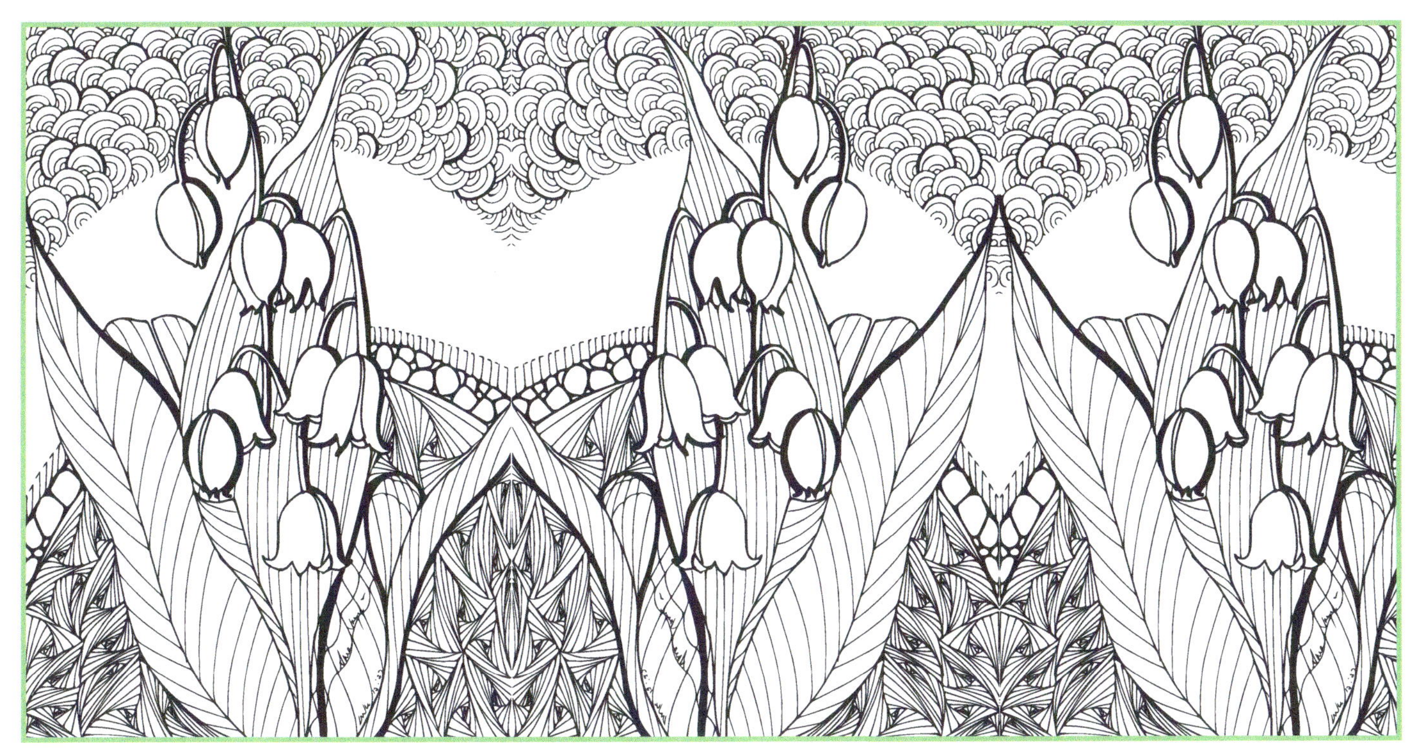

I Stand Me Tall

I stand me tall like the lily fair

Of the kingdom of God I am an heir

On this day may I cease from strife

To gratefully enjoy this blessed life

An heir to peace, joy, and love

No toil was ever sent from above

Outside this kingdom trouble lurks

But within I rest from all my works

"And if ye be Christ's, then are ye Abraham's seed,

and heirs according to the promise." Galatians 3:29

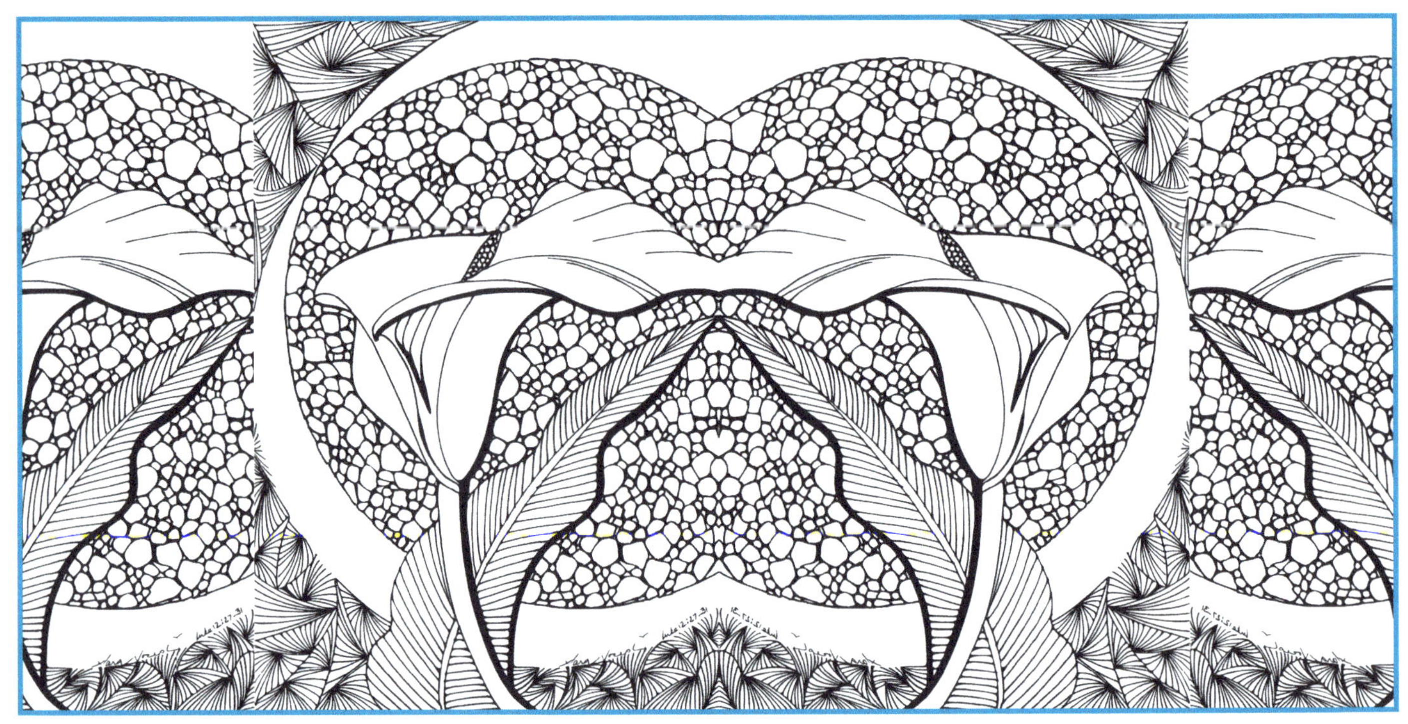

The End of This Journey, The Rest of Your Life

As you "Consider the Lilies" for the last time in this journal, I pray that you have anchored in your spirit these powerful truths from God's Word. Faith in Him is the *only* antidote for all anxiety, fear of the future, struggle, and stress. Faith in His ability and desire to bless you is all you need to live victoriously. You are an heir of a truly amazing kingdom. Now live like one!

Truth is always elegantly simple. Trust God, depend upon Him, obey His Word, and look to Him in faith for every aspect of your life. Then He promises to bless and care for all your needs. As a witness to His unfailing love, I testify to His faithfulness.

What we perceive with our five senses tends to crowd out the spiritual reality of God's Word. As you now know well, that is why Jesus pointed to the lilies of the field, giving us an unforgettable image of how to live. Choose to remember the lessons they so eloquently teach. In this journal, while thinking upon His words, you have engaged your visual and tactile senses with the form of the lilies as you colored. Some of those domineering senses were surely tamed by the truth.

I trust that your spirit is now stronger than when you began. When you falter in faith, may the Holy Spirit remind you of this journey.

Developing faith in God is priceless. Only when nurtured over time does it result in experiencing the kingdom that Jesus talks about. You have participated in that process by completing this coloring journal.

Real life is tough, but God can change those realities if you but trust Him to do so. May these truths that you have hidden in your heart remind you to yield to Him and His ways instead of attempting the futility of a struggle all alone.

Thank you for joining me on this journey. I hope you've learned much and enjoyed the process.

If this book was a blessing to you, would you please consider rating and reviewing it on www.amazon.com and www.goodreads.com? I would be most grateful.

ABOUT THE AUTHOR

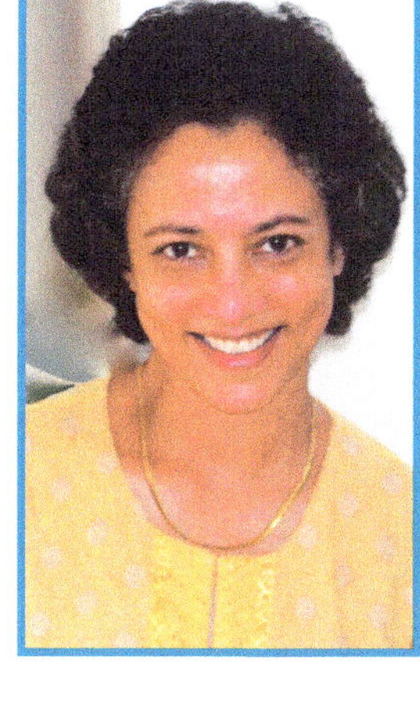

Sara Joseph is a painter, sculptor, and writer. Her art, created in watercolor, ink, oils, acrylic and polymer clay, is found in numerous corporate and private collections around the world.

Born in India, her early art training exposed her to the artistic traditions and rigor of the East. She immigrated to the United States with her husband, Jacob, and raised two sons, Johann and Reuben. A resident of Fort Worth, Texas, she is the author of the Christian Artist Resource website, an online resource for Christian artists internationally as well as a changing gallery of her own contemporary Christian art.

"Regardless of the medium I use," she says, "if the content is without meaning, I feel I've missed an opportunity that I may never get again—an opportunity to testify to the love of Jesus, the goodness of God, and the power of the Holy Spirit."

So with conscious intent, Sara works at translating her human experience into multiple media to best express the good news from the Bible that she has only one lifetime to tell.

Her book, ***Gently Awakened: The Influence of Faith on Your Artistic Journey,*** was the 2014 Readers' Favorite International Book Award Gold Medal Winner for Christian Nonfiction and Illustration.

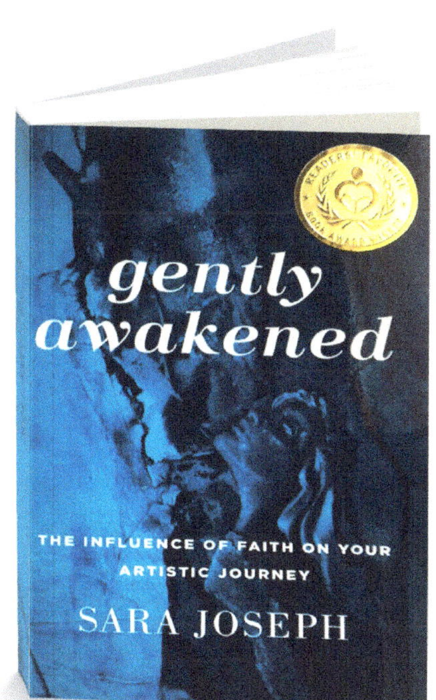

It is available on the Christian Artist Resource website, Amazon, Barnes and Noble and other retail bookstores.

Visit her at www.christian-artist-resource.com to view her art and to stay informed about her latest projects.

REVIEWS

"**Gently Awakened** *converts the hearts of readers as it covers deep terrain of faith, theology, salvation, beauty, and creativity in an engaging and personal manner.*

This is a book that needed to be written and should be widely read." Marisa Martin, columnist, *World Net Daily*; visual artist

"*This beautifully crafted book, illustrated in more ways than one with her own works, is an encouragement to recognize art in all its many forms as a divine calling.*

Each sentence is a masterpiece of expertly selected words reflecting a lightness of spirit which is uplifting, illuminating and 'gently awakening.'" Linda Caddick

"*Elegant, honest, and profound. Joseph's prose, verse, and artwork are delicious, but this book is more than that. She speaks into the tension where Christian artists dwell and guides to a deeper understanding of both the role art is meant to play in the lives of Christians, and the role Christians are meant to play, artistically, in our culture.*" Kit Tosello

CPSIA information can be obtained
at www.ICGtesting.com
Printed in the USA
FSOW03n0604130416
19096FS

9 780997 367300